"Secrets" of England

Colin Joyce

NHK Publishing

"Secrets" of England

Copyright ©2019 by Colin Joyce
ISBN978-4-14-035163-5 C0082
All rights reserved. Published in Japan
by NHK Publishing, Inc. (NHK Shuppan)

No part of this book may be used or reproduced
in any manner whatsoever
without written permission,
except in the case of brief quotations embodied
in critical articles and reviews.

For information:
NHK Publishing, Inc. (NHK Shuppan)
41-1 Udagawacho, Shibuya, Tokyo, 150-8081, Japan
http://www.nhk-book.co.jp

Printed in Japan

Foreword

A few years back, I was presented with a bit of a challenge. "Would you write a monthly column about Japan and England?"

It was the "and" that worried me.

I had written about Japan, of course, when I lived there as a Tokyo-based journalist. I had written about England after my return to my home country. And I had written about New York during the three years in between when I lived there. All three had their difficulties but the task was basically pretty clear. I wasn't so sure about how to write about "Japan and England" together.

Nevertheless, I decided to try. This book is

the fruit of my imperfect labours. The pieces within were written over a period of about three years for the monthly magazine, *NHK Radio Eikaiwa* Text. Fortunately for me, my editors weren't too pedantic about what constituted a column on Japan and England.

Sometimes I wrote about Japan from a British point of view. Sometimes I wrote about something in Britain that might be of interest to Japanese people. Since readers of the magazine are studying English, I wrote a few times about language: whether it be aspects of English that I think are interesting or my experiences learning Japanese.

Other times I just wrote about me, what was on my mind, or what I had been up to. My excuse for this is that I am English but much influenced by Japan, so I myself am suited to the topic.

I tried (as best I could) to "compare" Japan and England (when I could) as that is what my editors had asked me to do. I notice in retrospect that I used the words "chalk and cheese" a few times over the span of the three years. I guess that means I didn't find it straightforward.

I doubt I have successfully pinpointed the crucial differences and illuminated the key similarities between the peoples and cultures of Britain and Japan. The truth is that I haven't exactly endeavoured to do that. This isn't meant to be a definitive work of comparative culture or even my solemn thoughts on a serious subject. Naturally, I hope there are some insights and that perhaps some people will be guided towards a better understanding of Britain, or that they will see Japan in a different light. But more often than not I was trying to be diverting rather than highbrow.

This book appeared in Japanese first, published last year under the title of *Mind the Gap*. I am grateful to Noriyuki Miyagawa, Wataru Suzuki and Taeko Kajihara for their work on that edition and to Keita Harashima for his help in preparing this English language version.

Their cooperation has been invaluable. Any remaining errors, repetition of ideas or poor jokes are entirely my fault.

As we were finishing the Japanese edition, my friend Sharon Muir passed away after a long illness. She was a great bibliophile, librarian, wife, mother and friend. I was lucky to know her and was the grateful recipient of her kindness and hospitality on many occasions. I really wish I could pay her back and now I never can.

Contents

Foreword 3

1 Words for Uncommon Situations 10

2 Mind the Gap(s) 15

3 Party On, Japan! 23

4 The Treasures of British Cuisine 29

5 Ten Japanese Myths 35

6 "Secrets" of the English 42

7 A Sniffer's Guide to Japan 48

8 To Be in England in the Summertime 55

9 The Japanese Have a Word for It 62

10	The Things They Ask	70
11	Miscellaneous Strange Habits of the English	76
12	Surprise Surprise	83
13	The London Olympic "Debacle"	89
14	Keeping It Brief	96
15	The Japan I Didn't Like	102
16	Perplexities of British Life	108
17	A Journey into Japanese	115
18	"Sort of" Equivalents	122
19	Help! I Am Turning into a Trainspotter	128

Contents

20 Best of British Manners — 135

21 Japanglophilia Cafe — 141

22 A Collection of Collectives — 148

23 The (Unexpected) Dividends of Thrift — 153

24 The Juror Experience — 160

25 The *"Yuru-kyara"* Challenge — 169

26 "The Wetherspoons Brexit Test" — 177

Notes — 186
Afterword — 200
Profile — 205

本文に ＊マークのある語に関しては、
Notesのページ(p.186-198)に
簡単な説明があります。

Chapter
1

Words for Uncommon Situations

I like to invent words. I do it on purpose usually but also by accident occasionally.

Sometimes I infer* a non-existent word from an existing one. For example, there is a word "apologist" which means "someone who tries to excuse inexcusable behaviour". So I decided that there must also be an adjective "apologistic" but no such word exists, apparently.

Occasionally I try to use a sophisticated word and get it wrong. Lachrymose, derived from Latin, is an adjective meaning "tearful" or "prone to* crying". But I came out with "lachrymonious" instead. I think I mixed it together with the word "acrimonious", which is used to describe a dispute that is bitter and angry. So I decided it was a new word: a lachrymonious person would be someone who uses tears as a weapon in an argument.

Other times, I stumble across* a clever way of saying something. The other day I told a friend that something is "new and unique". So I decided to add: "It's 'newnique' so to speak."

I lived in Japan for a long time but now live in England. I am a sort of "Japanified" Englishman (note the new word!) As such, I find myself in certain situations that very few people do and, naturally, there are not always words for these rare situations.

So recently I have been trying to make up new words to fill the hole. I am not sure how successful I have been; some of them strike me as rather weak. But I want to introduce some of them anyway.

When I shake hands with someone I am meeting for the first time, I get a bit nervous and unconsciously bob* my head in a sort of mini bow. English people don't dip their heads in such situations, but I notice one of my old friends who also lived in Japan does it too. I decided to call this "bow-handing". (I derived the word from "glad-handing", which is used when a politician goes around shaking hands with everyone in an attempt to win popularity.)

I drink tea about five times a day. I like Japanese (green) tea but I prefer English tea. I have a supply of both in my kitchen but when I go to make the tea, I find I *always* have a slight preference for English tea. In other words, I will make English tea five times out of five if I just think "what do I want?" But then I stop and think to myself "sometimes I should have green tea for variety... I always enjoy it when I do have it... Japanese tea is healthier..." But *then* I think "right now, I would really love a cup of English Breakfast tea". So I get stuck* for several minutes. This I have decided to call "hesiteation" (i.e. hesitation over tea).

In Japan, I often hit my head as I go through doors. I am tall and Japanese doorways are too low. When I return to England from Japan, for the first few weeks I find myself unconsciously stooping* every time I walk through doors, even though English doorframes are high enough. I call this "redunducking" (from "redundant", or unnecessary, and "ducking").

The Japanese take their shoes off quite a lot: when they enter a house, before they enter a changing room etc. But the English don't usually do this. I sometimes get mixed up. In Japan, for example, I might take my shoes out of my locker at the gym and put them on right away rather than carry them to the exit and then put them on. (I wouldn't forget on the way in as there are visual clues to remind me: a step, a sign or a shoehorn.) In England, on the other hand, I instinctively take my trainers* off when I use the mats for stretching at the gym and am horrified* when other people don't. I call this situation "confu-shoe-sion".

In Britain, if you are given bread with a meal the bread will be placed at the back behind your main dish. When a meal is presented in Japan, the rice bowl is front and centre with other dishes around it. I noticed that I and most other Westerners in Japan will automatically move the big plate of fish to the middle and put the rice at the edge behind it. I call this "rear-ricing".

I like Japan and I like England. I wouldn't say, however, that I wish I could live my whole life in Japan (I would miss England) or that I am really proud of England (I am often disappointed and annoyed by it). I like having both countries in my life and, as a writer, my subject is often the differences and similarities between England and Japan. So I thought I was not quite a Japanophile and not exactly an Anglophile but a mixture: a "Japanglophile". So I have written this book in the spirit of "Japanglophilia". I hope you enjoy.

Chapter
2

Mind the Gap(s)

"People watching" is one of the most interesting things that you can do that doesn't cost money. I enjoy observing people: looking for their individual quirks* but also trying to spot which habits are common in which countries.

During the many years I lived in Japan, I watched out for distinctive behaviour. But I also became accustomed to Japan, so behaviour that might be unusual began to seem normal to me—and so I didn't notice it anymore. When I left Japan, and began to watch the Americans and the English, I was able to notice more sharply what behaviour was particular to Japan.

For example, Japanese people are particularly punctual. If a party starts at 8pm, people arrive at that time. When I was in New York,

I once arrived at a party 20 minutes "late" but found I was the first guest to arrive and the hostess was still busy preparing. It was quite embarrassing as I hardly knew her. Her best friends came about 15 minutes later and other guests came half an hour after that. In the US and Britain, it seems it is actually bad manners to arrive promptly for a house party unless specifically requested.

When I am in Tokyo, I notice that women tend to hold their handbags in the crook of their arms*. Men sometimes drag their heels, making a scraping sound as they walk. Young men sometimes wear a bunch of keys attached to a belt loop in their trousers*, which makes a jangling sound. (Very often, a man with a noisy bunch of keys ALSO scrapes his heels.)

I am not saying that *all* Japanese people have the same habits. Nor do I mean you never see these things in other countries. I mean that there are certain types of behaviour that are more prevalent* in Japan and that I associate with Japan.

On more than a couple of occasions I have heard a Japanese woman say that she got a little bit drunk *and then cleaned the apartment.* It interested me because when English people get drunk they tend to make a mess: leave empty bottles around, eat packets of crisps and drop crumbs* everywhere or fry food and leave the greasy pans unwashed. My only explanation is that Japanese people are not only tidy but consider cleaning a form of stress relief. So the same thing that causes them to drink too much causes them to start cleaning.

I dislike carrying lots of change so when I go to the shops I try to pay using as many coins as I can. This is always understood by Japanese cashiers. If my shopping comes to 3,803 yen and I give 4,303 the cashier will give me a single 500 yen coin in change. But in England and America, it sometimes causes confusion. If I need to pay £4.09 and I give £5.10 sometimes the cashier tries to return the "excess"

10 pence coin before giving me 91 pence in change (at least four more coins).

Unusually, it was permitted until recently for people to cycle on the pavement in Japan, and many people still do so. This may be one reason why more people cycle in Japan. In Britain, cycling is mostly for young people and is usually for commuting or for leisure, not to go to the shops or around town. Cyclists in Britain—almost without exception—have front and rear lights and will wear a helmet; Japanese often don't bother. Japanese cycle more slowly, on average. But most unusual is the way that some older women jump off their bike rather than applying the brakes.

In Japan, everyone has a stand for their bike—which almost no one does in Britain. Japanese use these to park their bikes side by side in neat rows, rather than leaning them against walls and rails and other bikes as in Britain.

But then when Japanese return to their

bikes, they wheel them out backwards, without looking, into the path of any oncoming pedestrians*. I had to sidestep reversing bicycles several times a month in Japan, and never once in England.

This may seem like a strange thing to mention but sometimes tour buses in Japan have karaoke facilities but no toilet. This amazed me the first time I experienced it. "For Japanese the urge to sing is more urgent than the need to use the toilet," I jokingly told my friends.

The manners of the *sento* (public baths) are quite distinctive but they also seem sensible to me once you learn them. What strikes me as interesting is that it is also commonplace for strangers to strike up conversation with each other at *sento* while completely naked. Westerners must be more prudish* because we tend even to avoid eye contact in saunas and changing rooms—and would not usually start chatting.

I have observed that some Japanese men shave differently from us: they shave "vigorously"* running the razor up and down over the same spot and even shaving their foreheads and temples (which I don't think require shaving). In Britain, we are told to shave "smoothly", trying to catch the bristles* with long, single strokes always downward.

The J-League is very interesting to me. Fans cheer their teams constantly and are generally polite to opposition teams. In England, fans chant insulting things about their opponents and make rude gestures. They also moan* and criticise their own players when they are not performing well or make mistakes. I like the Japanese version of football but sometimes it is confusing. Once, I wasn't concentrating and didn't notice that my team had won a penalty. The fans were cheering loudly all the time so there was no "crescendo" when we reached a dramatic moment.

The Japanese have rather chaotic offices.

Desks and cubicles are often piled with papers and books to an amazing degree. I have seen desks where I cannot see a space to put a computer.

I quite often see women office workers with a small blanket across their laps, which I never see in England. Maybe that's why there is no straightforward English word for what Japanese call *hiza-kake*. So it seems Japanese women feel the cold more. (Is that why the train carriages are so hot?)

I guess Japanese women must have a very sensitive sense of smell because sometimes they keep a handkerchief held to the nose on the train. Just by the way, sometimes when I get on a Japanese train there is a slight smell that I suspect Japanese people don't notice: it's a smell like the steam that comes out of a rice cooker just as the rice is nearly cooked.

I noticed also that many Japanese don't hold onto the straps when standing on a train, even if the train is crowded and moving fast.

It was some years before I heard that this is the result of a phobia because people think the handles on the straps are germ-laden*. I tend to associate people falling onto me on trains with Tokyo rather than London.

Chapter
3

Party On, Japan!

Japanese people sometimes ask me if we have cherry trees in England. In fact, we had one in our garden when I was a boy. I can vividly remember noticing how beautiful it was one day and asking my mum about it. She taught me a new word—blossom—and told me that it appears in spring. At the time, I thought that since spring lasts for a few months that the blossom would also last for two months or more. But then one day, all too soon, I would go into the garden and find the blossom had gone.

I remember that tree well, partly because while climbing it I got stung* by a bee for the first and only time. But we never had a picnic under it, hardly even sat under it and I don't think we ever took a picture of it in bloom in all the years we lived there. Having lived in

Japan and enjoyed many "hanami" seasons, I now regret not making more of our cherry tree.

This got me thinking about some of the things that Japan does better than England. Of course, cherry blossom viewing is one of the main ones. We have pleasant picnics in England when the weather allows (and sometimes even when it is rather cold). But nothing quite matches the national mood of celebration created by the cherry blossom in Japan. There is an intensity* about that short period that makes my heart beat a little faster. I can remember one year really praying that it would not rain at the weekend, as I knew it would be my only chance for hanami that year. Whereas in England, I might hope that the weather was nice for a picnic but I would be thinking that I could always do it another time if it rains.

However, my favourite eating experience in Japan is not hanami picnics but a warm, cozy* "nabe" party. The only piece of electronic equipment I brought back to England from Japan is my electric nabe. I think what I like about nabe parties is that everyone helps with the preparation and that the preparation time is part of the party. People sit around the nabe cutting up the food and throwing it into the pot as needed. Usually in England almost all the work is done alone by the host before the guests arrive. It must be quite tiresome*. I can remember parties where the host is really anxious, asking if there is enough food and worrying whether everyone is enjoying his or her efforts. I think a nabe party is more collegial and less stressful. Also, importantly for someone bad at cooking like me, it's hard to make bad nabe as long as the ingredients are reasonably fresh. There isn't much skill to it yet it's delicious.

One of my English friends also used to live in Japan and he has this joke I enjoy. When we meet and have a drink or dinner in London, even if it is just the two of us, at the end he says "hai" and stands up and starts to clap. It's the little clapping ceremony that Japanese use to formally end a party. Both my friend and I initially found this Japanese custom a bit funny, particularly as the party often carried on for a while afterwards or at least some people would go on to a second party. But we both got used to it and now I think that having everyone stop and do something as a group is a nice way to mark an occasion before people go on their way. It's a little bit more cheerful than the way I notice a lot of parties ending in England; which is that I look around and realise that many people have left after saying a few goodbyes and that now the room is half empty.

The other thing that I really miss about Japan is the various free festivities that there are to enjoy. The summer fireworks are particularly impressive. Tokyo Bay is my favourite but I also remember happily watching fireworks from the beach in Zushi. In England, fireworks events are held in November and I can remember shivering* with cold and wanting to go back inside while I watched some rather limp* fireworks fizzle* and pop.

I love the Oeshiki at Ikegami Honmonji temple; the incredible procession with drums and music that goes on for hours. The Awa Odori festival is the most memorable I have ever attended (I went three times and never bored of it). Yasukuni Shrine has some of the best events in Tokyo and is very accessible. I am always struck by how well organised and peaceful such large-scale events are.

But some of the festivals I have most enjoyed are ones I just chanced upon; little neighbourhood events where people of all ages dress up in colourful kimono, dance or sing or just wander around eating and drinking. I have sometimes sat alone at such festivals and been happy to experience that sense of community that still survives in Japan.

All in all, I think Japan is a very good place to have a good time.

Chapter
4

The Treasures of British Cuisine

English food has a poor reputation and I was often told so when I was in Japan. Japanese food, of course, has an excellent reputation and many people who visit Japan from overseas do so partly because they want to experience Japanese cuisine. So it's rather ironic that when I last visited Japan I found myself packing my suitcase with many different kinds of British food to give to friends and colleagues, or to eat myself.

In other words, I am a fan of English food. I miss it when I can't get it and I also enjoy sharing it with people who otherwise might not try it. I couldn't list all the best food from Britain but these are a few that I recommend.

I brought Hobnob biscuits to give to friends. These are a particularly luxurious biscuit topped with* rich chocolate on oatmeal. They are a notoriously "moreish"* food (i.e. you always want one more) so I warn people to limit themselves to two at a time. Britain has a strong tradition of biscuits—they are often served with tea—and we have many different varieties. Simple digestive biscuits are the most enjoyable for me, but other people like Bourbons (a cheap, chocolate "sandwich" biscuit) or shortbread. Another favourite is Jaffa Cakes, a light wafer with orange jelly and chocolate.

For myself, I brought oatmeal to make for breakfast. I don't think there is any food as perfect as oatmeal. It's cheap, simple to prepare, nutritious and tasty. It's also easy to digest, which is great for me as I sometimes have little appetite in the morning. I usually mix in some banana, a dash of* milk and some seeds to give it a bit of crunch.

Marmalade is a Scottish invention but it's eaten widely across Britain. I brought two jars to give away but ended up eating one myself. I particularly like "rough cut" marmalade, which contains some orange peel, and marmalade made from Seville oranges*, which has a slight bitterness that complements the sweetness. Recently I tried marmalade made with whisky and found it to have an interesting flavour (even though I dislike whisky itself).

Condiments* are a good thing to carry because just a little can transform meals several times. Sarsons vinegar is a product found in almost every English house. It has a strong malty flavour and I love the aroma that it gives when splashed on hot food. It's particularly good on chips but it can be used on any food that's a little oily (fried fish or chicken, for example).

I also brought a jar of Branston pickle, which is a chunky* relish* in a tangy* sauce. This can be added to sandwiches to enhance the flavour. It's particularly good with cheese or ham, especially if the cheese has a bland* flavour.

Actually, good strong cheddar cheese is one of the things I miss when I am away from England for a long time. In England, mature cheddar isn't very expensive but in Japan the best cheddar I found was bland and expensive. In the same way, I miss bacon rashers*. Somehow, the stuff we get in England is much tastier.

I bring English tea to give away and to use myself. At the moment, I am in love with the Assam tea from Waitrose supermarket because it never fails to give a good strong brew*. I can live without the "gourmet" teas such as Earl Grey or Darjeeling as long as I have had a nice cup of Assam to start the day.

British beer is different from beers you find in other countries. Not everybody likes it. Some Japanese friends are put off* by the lack of bubbles (most English beers are not carbonated*) and Americans sometimes complain

Things to pack for Japan

that it is "warm" (English beers taste best at cellar temperature, not heavily refrigerated). But there are many varieties of historic beers in Britain which I enjoy with food or without. When I am away from England, I often find myself craving* Old Speckled Hen which is a lovely beer, both smooth and bitter.

Unfortunately, it doesn't make much sense to bring bottles of beer in a suitcase. They are heavy and breakable; and even if I bring one or two they "disappear" all too soon. So I might instead pack a bottle of Pimm's No. 1, the famous summer spirit, or a bottle of Stone's Ginger Wine, spicy and refreshing, or a bottle of vintage Port, sweet and rich. All of these excellent drinks were invented by the English (although Port wine is produced in Portugal).

If I am travelling anywhere near Christmastime, I will be sure to bring a Christmas pudding. It's a rich, spicy* pudding that is traditional in England. It may be rather heavy to carry but it's worthwhile because it's so dense that you only need to eat a little, so a single pudding can be shared between six people.

I don't really feel insulted when people say that British cuisine is poor. Mostly, I just wish they knew what they are missing.

Chapter
5

Ten Japanese Myths

It seems that people in every country have certain wild* ideas. The British think that they have terrible weather, when in fact theirs isn't really a cold country and has lovely summers. The Americans—or some of them, at least—seem to think they invented democracy. Japan has quite a few delusions and I have been variously bemused*, amused and frustrated to learn them.

Japan is a small country. I have heard this many times and I remember reading once that a foreign correspondent was told by a Japanese man that he must be "a specialist in small countries" because so far he had been posted to Belgium, Singapore and Japan. Of course, Japan is very large compared to those places and is only "small" compared to the US or China. When someone says to me that Japan is small, I usually say: "Yes, only double the size of the UK!" Japanese are often surprised to hear that. I would say the correct sentence is: Japan is a medium-sized country.

Japan has four seasons. Almost every foreigner who goes to Japan gets told this and they don't know how to respond. I initially thought it must be the start of a joke, but no punchline came. (My own delusion was that all countries have four seasons; it never occurred to me that some places have little variation throughout the year.) But many Japanese apparently think Japan is the only place with four seasons, when in fact it is very common. I wouldn't even say that when I lived in Japan I found the seasons to be clearly defined. In Tokyo there is not as much green space as other places I have lived so I didn't see the changes in nature. It's hot in summer but otherwise the temperature is fairly even. So: Like many other countries, Japan has four seasons.

Japan has four seasons. I know that I wrote this above but I find it strange for another reason: Japan has a rainy season (*tsuyu*). Japanese people laugh at me when I mention this, saying that it's just "part of summer". I would say that the weather is significantly (even dramatically) different from the period before and the period that comes after, and it lasts for several weeks so it's a season of sorts. So: Japan has four main seasons.

Japan is crowded. Japan has a lower population density than many other countries. People usually point out that it is less densely populated than the Netherlands (a country that doesn't seem crowded at all). Interestingly, it is also less crowded than my own country, England (which is different from the UK as a whole) and the population of England is still rising rapidly. So I would say: Japan seems very crowded because so much of its population is crammed into the big cities and their surrounding areas.

Japan is crowded because it is so mountainous and those regions are uninhabitable. Japan is certainly mountainous. When I am flying over Japan I am often amazed at the extent of the forested mountains. But I am not convinced that it is *impossible* to live in mountainous places. I believe the Italians do, for example, though of course I don't mean atop* the big mountains. Japan also has quite a lot of countryside but people don't want to live there for a number of cultural and economic reasons. So: Japan's cities are very crowded because that's where people live in disproportionate numbers.

Japan and the UK are similar. I like the idea that Japan and the UK are sister nations, as both countries are very important to me (that's why I made up the word "Japanglophilia"). But I don't think you would find many British people who think this. It's true that we are island nations, constitutional monarchies*, somewhat aloof from the continents we inhabit, (supposedly) polite peoples... But this is "cherry picking" your arguments. I could easily find dozens of ways in which the Japanese and British are profoundly different. Or I could equally find ways in which the British and Germans are alike (fond of football, beer and meat dishes, Anglo-Saxon roots etc.) So: Japan and the UK have some surface similarities.

Japanese is an exceptionally difficult language. It's very hard to know how difficult it is to learn your native language because you didn't study it yourself so much as "picked it up" as a child. It doesn't surprise me that Japanese think their language is very difficult for three reasons. One, not many foreigners speak it very well. Two, foreign people will often say how hard Japanese is. And three, the part that Japanese people did study—learning to write kanji characters—is indeed very difficult. In fact, in some ways Japanese is a very logical language (very few irregular verbs, for example) and its pronunciation is not hard. Some parts are easy (no need to learn the singular and plurals of nouns) and some parts are hard (not just the writing). I found Japanese difficult but mainly because I am not good at learning languages. So: Japanese can be a difficult language.

Japan has regional dialects. This is true but, as with the "four seasons" delusion, it's not unique or even particularly rare. Scottish people speak differently from English. People from North East England speak very differently from Londoners. Of course, some of the dialects of Chinese cannot be understood by Chinese from other regions so in comparison neither Japan nor England is extraordinary. I also think Japanese exaggerate the extent of the regional differences. Apart from a few local words, Hiroshima speech seems very close to regular Kansai dialect. I admit, of course, that Aomori speech is really something unlike Tokyo speech (to the point that I struggle to understand it). So: Japan has interesting regional variations in speech, like many other countries.

Japan is a safe country. Let me put it this way: In England, we have no volcanoes, no earthquakes, no tsunamis and no typhoons. We have no bears (or any other dangerous wild animals). We have very few snakes, of these very few are poisonous and these are only mildly poisonous. I have never had my umbrella stolen in England. So: England is a safe country (?)

Japan is a very expensive country. Not only Japanese people say this; it is a kind of accepted truism. I think it was true 20 years ago but deflation has brought a lot of things down in price while other countries (such as the UK) have seen prices rise steadily. Now, there are many things that are cheaper—or at least better value—in Japan than England. It's cheaper to get a haircut in Japan, or stay in a basic hotel but more expensive to buy beer from the supermarket. So: Japan used to be expensive.

Chapter
6

"Secrets" of the English

There are certain things that you are only likely to know if you live in a country for a while. A tourist wouldn't have much chance to observe them and even an eager student would not usually get to hear of them. Recently, I was thinking of some things that Japanese people would be unlikely to know about England.

One of the biggest television programmes in Britain is *Top Gear*, which was originally a show that just reviewed cars but has grown to be an expensive and elaborate chat show and travel show (with a car theme). The formula* has been copied all over the world and it was national news when the presenter was fired in 2015.

But *Top Gear* is nowhere near as popular as the comedy *Only Fools and Horses* (the last series ended in 1991 but repeats are still often broadcast). English people still talk about their favourite moments from the show, in which two hapless* brothers dream of becoming millionaires despite only having a market stall* and little business prowess*.

The English sometimes call someone a "plonker" (a gentle way of saying "idiot"). The term was popularised on *Only Fools and Horses*.

The English are famous for their love of tea but well over 90 percent of the tea they drink is made from tea bags put directly in the cup. Very rarely does anyone use loose tea leaves* and a teapot.

PG Tips is the most popular brand of tea, partly because of the long-running, massively successful advertising campaign featuring "talking" chimpanzees who drank PG Tips. (I don't like the taste of PG Tips but loved the adverts when I was a kid.)

When England are playing in the World

Cup, there is always a surge* in electricity usage at half-time because millions of people who are watching the game on television get up and put the kettle on to make tea.

Wearing white socks is considered very bad taste for men. It is associated with lower-class youths who are looking for trouble.

But the worst fashion crime is wearing socks with open-toe sandals. Nevertheless, quite a lot of middle-aged Englishmen do this.

A lot of English people lick their plates when at home, to get all the gravy, or lick the custard from their dessert bowls. Fortunately, no one does this at restaurants.

It is "conventional wisdom" in England that it is incredibly dangerous to have any alcohol when taking antibiotics. People think it can cause a fatal interaction*, though it is not the case. Doctors let people believe this because they think sick people shouldn't be drinking.

The British give medals to animals for

The prestigious Dickin Medal. The recipient is the dog, not the man.

heroism. The Dickin Medal has been awarded 69 times since it was introduced in 1943. Carrier pigeons have won it 32 times, dogs 32 times and horses 4 times. But my favourite is the only cat to have won it, Simon, who stopped an infestation* of rats on a damaged warship despite being badly injured himself.

The present-day English don't use umbrellas very often.

People think it is outrageous if there are no seats available and they have to stand on the train on the way to or from work. (Mind you, the trains are so expensive that people are entitled to expect a comfortable journey.)

There are many regional accents in England. People think the Birmingham accent sounds boring and the east London accent indicates someone is untrustworthy. The Yorkshire accent is generally thought to sound pleasant and trustworthy. People from west England tend to speak a bit more slowly than others. The dialect of Newcastle and the North East region is possibly the one most different from "standard" English.

English people are very bad at mimicking* Scottish accents.

People in England love hedgehogs. But the hedgehog population is falling at a dramatic rate and they may become extinct in the near future.

Red squirrels are outnumbered by* non-native grey squirrels by almost 20 to 1. A majority of English people have never seen an actual red squirrel. But if you ask a British person to draw a picture of a squirrel he will almost certainly draw a red squirrel.

Roads sometimes change names as they go along. In Colchester, where I live, Magdalen Street becomes Barrack Street and then becomes Hythe Hill in the space of less than a mile. But some road names change many times more than that.

Acacia Avenue is considered the most "average" (i.e. suburban, middle-class) street name in England.

One of the most popular formats for jokes is that "an Englishman, a Scotsman and an Irishman…" are confronted with a similar situation. In this joke, the Englishman is usually sensible*, the Scotsman may or may not be stingy* and the Irishman will do something stupid. Obviously, such jokes are demeaning* and stereotyping (but sometimes they are also quite funny).

Everyone in England thinks all of the above is common knowledge and normal behaviour.

Chapter
7

A Sniffer's Guide to Japan

People often talk about the amazing sights they have *seen*, especially when they travel abroad. They talk about the interesting things they *tasted* when they recall great meals. They go to concerts to *hear* wonderful music. But it is rare to hear people talk about the things they have *smelled*. In that way, smell is rather neglected among the five senses (along with touch) but it is more important than people realise. Our sense of smell somehow goes directly to parts of the mind and memory that other senses do not.

A person might, for example, smell lavender and immediately think of his grandmother because her house smelled of lavender. A friend of mine hated going into Japanese convenience stores in winter because of the steamy smell from the *oden* on the counter. It wasn't so much that he didn't like the smell but rather that it was the smell he associated with his first winter in Tokyo when he split up with his girlfriend and also had no money. The smell made him feel depressed, even years after he found a good job and a new girlfriend.

Some people have a very sharp sense of smell and others don't. I think I am somewhere in the middle but I do consciously make an effort to experience the "olfactory* world". In this column, I want to share some of my insights (or should that be "insmells"?)

Food smells are very common in Japan. It's not just *oden* in the convenience stores over the cold months. I associate summer in Tokyo with suddenly being hit in the face by a powerful blast* of garlicky smelling ramen. As I write this, I can remember it happening on a specific occasion in Meguro circa* 2000. (Bizarrely, I can even remember which trousers and shoes I was wearing, which is surely proof that smell is linked with the memory.) Stores in Japan deliberately pump* the smell of their food into the street as an advertisement. It depends on the person, I suppose, but in my view ramen smells the worst and eel (*unagi*) smells the best.

Another smell I associate with Japan is the combination of air-conditioning and tobacco. It's an odd smell because cigarette smoke is unpleasant but on a hot day the air-conditioning is alluring*. I used to notice it a lot in taxis but it's also there whenever I pass a pachinko parlour. Occasionally I smell it somewhere else and think, "Ah! The smell of pachinko."

There are smells I miss when I am in Japan. Chief among them is newly cut grass. It's a beautiful aroma but also when you smell it, it means you are in a place where thick green grass grows naturally. Grass doesn't smell much until it's cut in large quantities, so that smell is one you usually get only in a park in summer (when the grass grows too prolifically*). So it's a "happy place smell".

Another smell I truly love—and don't experience in Japan—is vinegar on chips. I stress that it isn't the smell of chips, or even the vinegar. It's the smell of the vinegar coming from hot chips. In Britain, people will often buy an "open" bag of chips from the fish and chip shop, splash vinegar on the chips and eat them walking down the road. The smell is almost intoxicating*, especially in winter. For me, it is "the smell of England".

If I were to rank my three favourite Japanese smells, in third place would be the smell of the steam from a rice cooker just as the rice is almost ready. It's not exactly the smell of rice itself, it's the slightly sharper smell of the steam. I am sure that I like the smell so much because of the anticipation I feel at that moment. When I smell it, it usually means I am about to eat and I am probably very hungry (as it takes quite a long time to cook rice). It's a bit like Pavlov's dogs.

Second place is the smell of *genmaicha*. I don't drink the stuff very often but I like the smell a lot. I first experienced it in the staff room of a Japanese school where I worked 20 years ago but, again, recalling the smell transports me back in time. In particular, I rate that smell highly because it helps me win an argument. I consider myself a lover of tea *over coffee*. But coffee lovers will often point out that coffee smells better than tea. They have a point. The tea we drink in England tastes superb but has only a very mild smell. When you step into a tea shop you aren't immediately struck by a delicious "tea smell" whereas coffee shops have a lovely, ambient* coffee smell. But, thanks to *genmaicha*, I can counter that argument by pointing out that some types of teas smell just as good as coffee.

My number one favourite Japan smell isn't very original: tatami. I keep a little square of tatami in a drawer in my house in England. Occasionally, I open that drawer and just inhale deeply. It's a very natural and calming smell. When I lived in Japan I always chose to rent apartments that had at least one tatami room and I definitely sleep more peacefully in a tatami room. I used to cycle past a tatami workshop on my way to work in Tokyo and it was one of the highlights of my morning commute. If I ever save enough money I want to convert my loft in my home in England into a tatami room. The ceiling (i.e. the roof of my house) is low so I will sit on cushions on the tatami mats around a kotatsu.

The sense of smell is mysterious because it is possible to come to like an unpleasant smell. I know this personally from living in Japan. I don't think anyone could claim that ginkgo nuts, fallen from the trees, is a nice smell. It stinks* like dog mess or rotten cheese and can be quite overwhelming when the stinky pulp is mashed up by people walking on them. But I enjoy this smell because I associate it with happy days in Japan, spent somewhere with trees and a bit of nature, and being out in the open air on a beautiful autumn day. A "good bad smell", if you follow me.

Chapter
8

To Be in England in the Summertime

As I write this, we are experiencing the hottest day for a decade in England. Men are walking around the town bare-chested*. People are complaining that they are "melting" and cannot sleep at night because it is "sweltering"*. The newspapers are full of news about the "heatwave". People are jumping into the fountain in Trafalgar Square to cool down. The train system is in chaos because the tracks have got too hot. The air-conditioning on the carriages cannot cope*; commuters are "boiling". In the afternoon, the temperature reached 35 degrees in places.

So it is hot, but not actually unbearably hot because it isn't very humid. I don't have air conditioning in my house or even an electric fan. I have instead opened the windows to let a breeze pass through. (In really hot countries, you should close the windows when it is hot.) I could sit in the garden in the shade, though I admit it would not be a good day for heavy gardening. I haven't broke into a sweat, don't need to drink cold water every 10 minutes and don't need to shower every hour. So, on even the hottest day in 10 years, I would say it is much nicer than the weather in Japan on most days from June to the end of August.

Moreover, I am looking forward to a long cool evening. In June and July it is still light outside until around 9pm, so when I finish work it will still be light enough to go for a walk in the park or sit in the garden and have a drink.

This got me thinking. Clearly, the English summer weather is much nicer than Japan (so 1-0 England!) but it's not just the weather that makes a great season. I decided to weigh up* the pluses and minuses of summer in England and Japan in a few other categories as well.

Secondly, (after weather) comes summer food. In my first year in Japan, a student told me that eating eel (*unagi*) in summer will give you stamina to battle the heat. I am not actually sure if it does but eel is so delicious that I don't need an excuse. Many Japanese think of watermelon as the classic summer food. I am not a big fan of watermelon as I can't stand having juice dribbling* on my hands and shirt but I have to say it's more exotic and tasty than the cucumber, which is one of the English summer staples*. Believe it or not, people here sometimes eat cucumber sandwiches, which seems unnatural to me. If you ask an Englishman to name a typical summer food, he will probably say strawberries and cream. This is a nice thing to eat but it's hardly high cuisine (plus we can get strawberries all year round in England now). So in this category Japan is a clear winner: 1-1.

Thirdly, drinks. Strawberries and cucumbers may not be all that exciting as food

"Summer in a cup"

but they are part of a classic English drink: Pimm's No. 1. This is a mildly alcoholic drink that we make in summer by mixing Pimm's with lemonade and then adding ice, mint and slices of strawberry, cucumber and apple. It's a bit spicy and very refreshing. People call it "summer in a cup". In Japan, people just drink beer in summer. Okay, beer tastes a bit better in summer but it's not a unique or special summer drink. In that sense, cold barley tea (*mugi-cha*) is more "summery" but it's not nearly as wonderful as Pimm's. So this is a victory for England (2-1).

Fourthly, sports. Summer means Wimbledon tennis in England, though famously no Englishman has won the men's singles since 1936. (Andy Murray won in 2013 but he is Scottish.) I have never actually been to Wimbledon so have only seen it on television. I admire the incredible prowess of the players but I cannot say I like tennis as a sport. It's a bit too mechanical* for my taste, in that the player who serves usually wins the game and the match is won by the player who breaks the other player's serve at an appropriate moment. In Japan, summer makes me think of the high school baseball at Koshien Stadium. I went to this several times and really enjoyed the atmosphere, which I found a bit surreal*. The standard of play is not fantastically high but the passion is very evident. It's quasi*-military at times and is played in horrible heat. For me, the school bands and the kids supporting are almost as important as the players. It's a real "experience" and very Japanese.

Comparing Wimbledon and Koshien is like chalk and cheese. They are so different that I can't say which one is better, though both have their pros and cons. So I would call this a draw and put the score at 2 ½ - 1 ½.

Fifthly, events. England has some iconic concerts such as Glastonbury, if you like rock and pop, and the very reasonably priced BBC proms at the fantastic Royal Albert Hall in London for classical music fans. There are also lots of little festivities such as bands playing in local parks or outdoor theatre and cinema. I don't think Japan has as many such events or ones that are quite as good. But, as I have written before, Japan is particularly blessed with wonderful festivals and the big summer fireworks are among the most enjoyable things I have ever experienced. If I were in Japan, I would definitely attend five or six summer events a year whereas in England I rarely bother. So that would bring the scores level.

Yet, in my mind, I already have a clear

preference. When I think of summer in England, my immediate thoughts are of sitting outside, enjoying our "green and pleasant land" and feeling more energetic. When I think of summer in Japan, I think first of my shirt sticking to my back because of sweat, of feeling dog tired, of desperately wanting to get home to get out of the heat only to find that it's hotter inside my apartment than outside until the air conditioning starts working. It seems that by breaking the question down into parts I am over-analysing. Instinctively, I just know I would rather be in England in summer.

Chapter
9

The Japanese Have a Word for It

One of the pleasures of learning a foreign language is that you discover there is a really good way of expressing some things that are clumsily* expressed in your native language. Sometimes, these words and expressions get adopted. In English, we sometimes say schadenfreude* (from German), plus ça change* (from French) or kismet* (from Turkish).

Not many words have been adopted from Japanese into English but I do try to tell people about certain ways of saying things that I find very useful or clever in Japanese.

Betsu bara is a particularly obvious one. The idea of a "second stomach" for sweet things is something that ought to have occurred to me before. Many times, people say they are "completely full" but then manage to eat ice cream. On those occasions, I tell them about their *"betsu bara"*.

Once, I was at a friend's house and their infant son was found in the other room taking tissues out of a box, ripping them up and throwing them around the room. Normal infant behaviour. But I almost burst out laughing when they said he's having a **matsuri**! I knew what a normal *matsuri* is: it's a festival. But it struck me as hilarious* to describe any sort of exuberant* behaviour this way. I now use this word a lot more. Now, when I drink too much it's a beer *matsuri*. Eating too much is a food *matsuri*.

I suppose I could say someone is "malfunctioning"* when he is behaving strangely but it doesn't seem quite as natural as saying "**kowareteiru**" in Japanese. I am not sure if this is standard Japanese but I have used it a few times and have heard it a few times. It doesn't seem too harsh* as it implies the strange behaviour is not the person's normal behaviour and that, possibly, he or she can be fixed.

I learned *u nomi ni suru* very early on, at the time I was just starting to study Japanese. I learned it because I wanted to know the Japanese for what I myself was doing: learning phrases to repeat without understanding the full meaning. That included this expression. *"u nomi ni suru" wo "u nomi ni shita"*, so to speak.

But it wasn't just a language problem. I didn't know at the time how cormorants* swallow a fish whole, in a dramatic gulp that looks rather comical (though I am sure it isn't funny for the fish). When I learned that, the brilliance of the expression became obvious.

Later still, I observed a cormorant with my own eyes catching and eating a fish in the Thames. First, the cormorant dives under the water and swims after a fish, taking the fish on in its own environment. Usually the cormorant surfaces thirty seconds or so later with nothing to show for his efforts, at a surprisingly distant spot. When he does eventually catch something, it isn't necessarily easy to swallow. He may have to toss the fish into the air several times to get it lined up nicely to slide down his gullet*. It seems a complicated operation. And that made me think that the expression had hidden depth: even learning by rote* can be a frustrating task requiring time and effort.

I am not alone among foreigners in finding it hilarious that Japanese say of something cute that **me ni irete mo itakunai**. What an idea: it wouldn't hurt if I put it in my eye. A native speaker of Japanese will have heard the expression many times, so it cannot be as fresh or as striking as it is to us foreigners hearing it the first time. Occasionally, in an attempt to give a Japanese person some idea of how funny it sounds, I rephrase it a bit. "*ano koinu kawaii desune… me ni iretakunatta!*" ("That's a cute puppy. I want to put it in my eye.")

An English grandmother might say to her cute granddaughter that "you're so sweet I want to eat you all up", which is roughly equivalent to *me ni irete mo itakunai*. But on the whole I think the Japanese is funnier (how could it not hurt?!) and the English a bit scarier. As a child I didn't think my nan* was going to eat me, but it was a bit worrying that it seemed to have crossed her mind.

When I lived in Ota City, I was rare among my Tokyo counterparts for having a garden. I proudly boasted of it to friends in England, adding that it was the size of a cat's forehead (**neko no hitai**), initially to their bemusement then to their amusement. No one ever got it immediately; no one ever failed to get it within a second or two. Proof, I think, that it hits a perfect spot by being clear but forcing people to focus on what is being said. "Small" wouldn't have done that.

In English, we could say it was the size of

a postage stamp and that is not a bad expression. But it's a bit obvious. It is a comparison with something small whereas the Japanese is a comparison with a small bit on a small thing (a cat). And also cats aren't noted for their small foreheads so it's not a lazy expression that draws on a well-known fact (such as, as big as an elephant). On the other hand it isn't obscure like "*neko-jita*": English people have to be *told* that cats flinch* from eating hot food so that term isn't evocative*.

For a while my favourite Japanese word was **aka-chan**. It struck me as really funny but accurate to call a small baby "red" and endearing* to add the diminutive suffix* "*chan*". I try to explain this to English friends and my approximate translation is "dear little red thing". Obviously, Japanese don't think about the word much but to an outsider it's hilarious.

Japanese is very rich in onomatopoeia* (*giseigo* and *gitaigo*). These have somehow attached themselves to my brain, though when I first encountered them they were just more "words to learn". Now, when I mention my friend's kid (with the tight curly hair) I want to say *"kurin!"* as if that was needed to explain. When I say around-and-around I want to add *"guru guru"* as if to complete the thought. When I hear an audience clap, all I hear now is *"pachi pachi"* not "clap clap clap". By coincidence, a few days after attending a very *"pachi pachi"* concert in London, I read a story in an English newspaper about onomatopoeia from around the world and the author finished by saying his favourite was *"pachi pachi"*.

I don't always *like* useful expressions. One that irritates me greatly is when a store is closed and the sign says "***tsugou ni yori...***" I suppose this would be "Due to unforeseen circumstances..." in English but the Japanese is vaguer. It doesn't actually commit to *any explanation at all*. It doesn't say "we are sick" or "the kitchen caught fire". It doesn't even claim that something very difficult or wholly unpredicted has happened. It annoys me when I see it but I would dearly love to use it the next time I miss my deadline.

Similarly, I see that **shikata ga nai** is useful but is used too much. It can be a good expression when there really is "nothing to be done" about a situation and it must be endured. But sometimes people use it in Japan when there *is* an alternative and it just suits them not to consider it. Sometimes, when I have complained about unfair and unreasonable situations I have been told *"shikata ga nai"*. On those occasions, I cannot help but think it translates as "shut up and go away".

That is why I invented an expression that I want Japanese to adopt and use sometimes in response: *"**shikata ga aru!**"*

Chapter
10

The Things They Ask

To many foreign people, Japan is a distant land. For Westerners, it's not just geographically far away, it's a place that they know very little about. This makes people both simultaneously* ignorant and curious. So people like me, who have lived in Japan for a long time, get asked a lot of questions about what it is like. Sometimes, the questions are intelligent and make me think again about Japan, but other times I find them silly (I was once asked if there are swimming pools in Japan, for example).

Here are a few of the most common questions I have been asked over the years (mostly by British friends) along with some comments and the answers that I might give. I imagine Japanese people who go overseas will get asked similar questions—and may have different answers.

Is it true that they pay people in white gloves to push commuters onto trains?

Somehow, this image of Tokyo rush hour gets shown on television occasionally and is very shocking and memorable to British people. I tell them it's true but I have never personally experienced it. (Then, they want to know why people endure it—and that's harder to answer.)

What are the differences between Chinese and Japanese people?

This is a huge and complex question. One strategy for evading it is to answer that, "They are about as different as British and Germans."

Have you ever met a geisha / sumo wrestler?

In my case, the answer is yes to both but I suspect that is unusual. You wouldn't normally just bump into* them in the street (except perhaps in Kyoto / Ryogoku).

Why do Japanese manga and anime characters look Western when they are "made in Japan"?

A difficult question for me, as I am not very interested in manga. I answer that that is the style of the genre and that, to fans, the characters don't look Western; they just look like anime and manga characters.

Why do Japanese write in "squiggles"* (i.e. kanji characters)?

"To make it really, really hard for foreigners to learn the language" I answer, because not that many people are really interested enough to listen to the full history of Japanese writing. If someone really wants to know, I might just give the short answer that "pictographs"* were used in many ancient languages around the world and that the alphabet ultimately derives from pictographs.

Is Japanese the most difficult language in the world?

Certain aspects of Japanese are very

difficult for a native speaker of English, "but then five-year-old Japanese children seem to manage to speak it".

How fast is the "bullet train"?

Very fast but not just fast. It's also comfortable, clean and very regular!

What is the religion of Japan?

A tricky one, as it is unusual for people in other countries to follow more than one religion in the way Japanese follow Buddhism and Shinto. And Japanese sometimes have Christian weddings even if they're not Christian…

Why do Japanese work so hard and is it true there is a special word for "working to death"?

There is such a word and there is a culture of hard work in Japan. It comes from a complex combination of historical, social and economic causes. But it would be wrong to think of Japanese as wild with enthusiasm for more and more work.

Japanese seem very shy and modest but then they seem to really "let go"* at karaoke. Why?

Karaoke is a special place in which it is permitted to be a bit wild and show off. It is a kind of release from everyday social conventions.

Do Japanese people use chopsticks for eating everything?

Actually, no. Western food is usually eaten with a knife and fork. But even some traditional food is not eaten with chopsticks. (I used chopsticks for fried rice for months before I noticed that Japanese people use a spoon.)

Why is Mount Fuji so important to Japanese?

Now, you can answer that it's not just important to the Japanese; it has World Heritage Status. Or you could explain that it has an extraordinary, majestic presence and is visible for many miles around on a clear day.

Are Japanese really polite all the time?

Japanese are really polite *most* of the time.

(Not all the time, and not all Japanese.)

Is it true that Japanese women and Japanese men speak different languages?

There are significant differences but it's still only slightly different versions of the same language. Even so, there is a potential for embarrassment if a foreign man learns Japanese from female Japanese friends.

(I am really sorry to report this last question to anyone working really hard at English, but I genuinely have been asked many times):

Japanese education is said to be very good, so why can't Japanese people speak English?

Good question...

Chapter
11

Miscellaneous* Strange Habits of the English

There are certain things about England and the English that I only noticed because I lived in Japan. That is to say, before I lived in Japan I thought certain behaviours were so normal or inevitable* that I paid no attention to them. Here are a few of the things that now surprise me about my countrymen having seen that things are different in Japan (and probably other countries too).

The English almost always pay for goods with a note. If something comes to £2.66 the English will pay with a £10 note. If it comes to £10.42, they will pay with a £20 note. Hardly anyone ever searches through their change to get rid of their coins. This has two notable consequences: shops are constantly running out of change and customers are constantly accumulating coins. (Both problems must have been worse before the spread of debit cards.)

A friend pointed out that one problem from going to the pub is that you leave with ridiculously heavy pockets because you go to the bar four or more times, paying with a note and receiving lots of coins in change each time.

Possibly, this is one reason why **the English drop coins all the time** (and don't pick them up). I almost never found coins on the floor in Japan but it is extremely common in England. You see coins on the floor in pubs, in the street and in changing rooms. When men take off their trousers, change often falls out. (I see it at the gym constantly.) Very often, men will not bother to pick the coins up. It's as if they don't think of coins as real money.

There are lots of beggars in England, including people who appear able to work. Only twice in all my time in Japan did someone beg money from me (Omiya 1995 and

Akihabara 2013) but it happens to me in England almost every day. Sometimes, I get asked for money five times in the same day. Sometimes, the same person asks me for money more than once at different locations in town. Typically, they ask for a specific sum of money: "40 pence for the bus" or "70 pence for a cup of tea". I think they do this because they know the English generally don't think of sums less than £1 as significant so are likely to give them some coins.

When it gets hot, **English men often take their shirts off.** They take off their shirts in the park or even when they are walking around town. Mostly young men do this but even some middle-aged men with big bellies* do it. It's not a pretty sight. In my town, there is one bar that has a sign saying "Shirts must be worn on the premises"*. When I first saw this sign, I assumed it meant "no T-shirts or football shirts" (some bars have dress codes like this). But it actually means "no bare chests".

accumulating coins. (Both problems must have been worse before the spread of debit cards.)

A friend pointed out that one problem from going to the pub is that you leave with ridiculously heavy pockets because you go to the bar four or more times, paying with a note and receiving lots of coins in change each time.

Possibly, this is one reason why **the English drop coins all the time** (and don't pick them up). I almost never found coins on the floor in Japan but it is extremely common in England. You see coins on the floor in pubs, in the street and in changing rooms. When men take off their trousers, change often falls out. (I see it at the gym constantly.) Very often, men will not bother to pick the coins up. It's as if they don't think of coins as real money.

There are lots of beggars in England, including people who appear able to work. Only twice in all my time in Japan did someone beg money from me (Omiya 1995 and

Akihabara 2013) but it happens to me in England almost every day. Sometimes, I get asked for money five times in the same day. Sometimes, the same person asks me for money more than once at different locations in town. Typically, they ask for a specific sum of money: "40 pence for the bus" or "70 pence for a cup of tea". I think they do this because they know the English generally don't think of sums less than £1 as significant so are likely to give them some coins.

When it gets hot, **English men often take their shirts off**. They take off their shirts in the park or even when they are walking around town. Mostly young men do this but even some middle-aged men with big bellies* do it. It's not a pretty sight. In my town, there is one bar that has a sign saying "Shirts must be worn on the premises"*. When I first saw this sign, I assumed it meant "no T-shirts or football shirts" (some bars have dress codes like this). But it actually means "no bare chests".

don't seem to mind. Rain is just water to them, so rain may delay the drying process but that's all. Even if it pours rain, they will just leave the clothes out until they dry the next day.

The English are very wasteful with water. It seems to me that Japanese are careful with water and I learned to be so too. Most notably, they use the same bath water for the whole family and sometimes even then use it to do the laundry. I thought it was clever that you could wash your hands with the water that was refilling the toilet. The English, however, seem to think there is an inexhaustible* supply of water. They will wash dishes from a running tap*; they leave the tap on while they brush their teeth; they soak* their gardens even when the weather forecast is for rain tomorrow; they will sometimes blow their nose on a tissue, throw the tissue in the toilet and flush it (instead of throwing it in the bin). Actually, I can remember doing all those things when I was younger and never thought about it at all. Believe it or not, I thought water was free (because it used to be included as part of local government tax and we didn't get a water bill).

When people come round my house (or when I am at their houses) I point out how much water they are using unnecessarily. Mostly, they look at me as if I am weird or perhaps call me a miser*. I can't help it though; I have been changed and can't go back.

Chapter
12

Surprise Surprise

Before I ever went to Japan, I had some idea of what to expect. I had read a couple of books on Japan, seen a few Japanese films. I had picked up some things unconsciously. Other information—a few choice things—I had learned from people who knew about Japan.

The problem was that what I knew was dwarfed by* the masses of things I didn't know and the number of assumptions I made that were totally wrong. Sometimes, I look back and laugh about the misconceptions I had about Japan. These are a few of my bigger surprises, in no particular order.

Japanese people drink quite a lot and can get raucous*. I had the idea that Japanese were very straight-laced* people: sober* and sensible*. I can vividly remember my sense of shock at seeing staggering* salarymen on the streets of Kobe on my first weekend in Japan. I would later find out that Japanese can be very boisterous* on occasions, quite demonstrative* and rather earthy in their humour. Big shocks all round.

Japanese food makes you put on weight. Or perhaps I should say it made *me* put on weight. I knew that the Japanese "fish and rice-based diet" was the healthiest in the world. In Japan, I immediately noticed how few people were overweight. But it didn't work out that way for me, for two reasons. Firstly, I wrongly assumed that all Japanese food was healthy. So my constant scoffing* of okonomiyaki and takoyaki turned out to have consequences. Secondly, when I did eat healthily (e.g. soba noodles) I would get really hungry soon after. I found it too easy to digest and some days I would fit in a whole extra meal.

Japanese television is mostly boring. When I was a kid, I loved *Monkey* (*Saiyuki*, in

Japanese) and *G-Force* (*Gatchaman*). So when I came to Japan I was expecting to find interesting television programmes. Instead, there were a lot of game shows—making people get into really hot baths was popular at the time—and shows in which the same five or six "tarento" made jokes while an audience of young girls laughed. Cheap, lowest common denominator television. I still get irritated when I see certain television personalities.

Not many Japanese people speak English. I had heard that Japan had an incredible education system and that students work very hard. There is a lot of truth in that but it doesn't seem to produce many people capable of speaking English. I honestly expected 90 percent of Japanese to speak English. I would say it's more like 10 percent and of those many didn't learn it at school. I don't really know why but it's pretty much the same in England, where very few people speak a foreign language despite studying at school.

Very few Japanese have been to England. Whenever I went to London, I would always see Japanese tourists. It was standard wisdom that the Japanese loved England. I concluded therefore that most Japanese had visited England at some point*. It didn't occur to me that even if there were hundreds of thousands of Japanese visitors every year for two decades that would still be only a small percentage of the population. In Japan, I often tried to start conversations with people by asking had they been to England before I realised it was usually a dead end*.

Japan doesn't have much grass. Wherever you go in England there is grass: in people's gardens, in school fields and in parks. I thought it was "nature's carpet" and it just grew everywhere naturally. I was shocked when I went to Japan and saw kids playing in grassless parks and boys playing football on dirt pitches*. I really, really missed grass and thinking about lush*, soft grass was one of the things that made me most homesick.

Japan isn't uniformly advanced. Japan has a reputation for being "futuristic". Some people think Japan has robot waiters and that there are robot pets in people's homes. In many ways, Japan is very advanced but it can also be quite backwards. I can remember that ATMs closed for Golden Week in my first year in Japan. ("Why do machines need a holiday?" I wondered.) That was 20 years ago but still in Japan people often have to pay to use an ATM or to transfer money. Getting a prepaid mobile phone when visiting Japan is an expensive nuisance*. And in Tokyo, the "24-hour city", all the trains stop around midnight. (In London, parts of the train and underground system are now 24-hour on weekends.) I could give more examples.

Learning Japanese was hard. This might sound obvious. I had heard that Japanese was a difficult language but I thought I was so clever that I would master it anyway in no time.

Instead, I found I had no talent for learning languages and it took me a long time and a lot of hard work. And I also realised that speaking Japanese is not as hard as people say. So that was two surprises really: that Japanese is not all that hard but I couldn't get the hang of* it anyway.

As the English say, it was "surprise surprise".

Chapter
13

The London Olympic "Debacle"

As Tokyo prepares for the 2020 Olympics, London 2012 is being held up as an example of a successful games. Certainly, Japan is wise to learn lessons from previous games and there are reasons why it is sensible to look at what London did. But it concerns me that London is being considered only as if it were a complete success.

I don't deny that certain aspects of the London games were successful. But those aren't what I want to focus on here. Rather, I want to flag up* some negative aspects to the London Olympics that Japan should be aware of and strive to avoid.

The Olympic Stadium was the centrepiece of the games. Its story is illustrative and infuriating. It was originally estimated to cost

£280 million but actually cost £429 million to build. However, it didn't end there because its future beyond the Olympics was not made certain. After the games a hugely expensive "retrofitting"*—another £272 million—was required to convert it into a football stadium while maintaining the athletics track.

Now, a stadium that cost taxpayers over £700 million is home to West Ham football club, leased to them for a one-off payment of £15 million and then £2.5 million a year. This represents an incredible bargain for the privately owned football club and a dreadful deal for the UK public. The London Legacy Development Corporation*, which handles the Olympics "legacy", tried to conceal many details of the deal with West Ham. It wasn't until* "freedom of information" legislation* was invoked* that we were able to discover certain facts. It turned out that, among other things, West Ham doesn't have to pay for the stewards* on match days, or even the corner flags used in games.

The London Olympics was supposed not just to be a sports event but a transformative event for London. There were infrastructure improvements (better public transport, for example, and a nice new park) but it is hard to see that it made any real dent* in the biggest problem facing London: the housing crisis. London housing has become incredibly expensive and ordinary people increasingly cannot afford to buy even a small apartment.

New housing has been built in the area of the Olympics Park but little of it is so-called "affordable housing"*, i.e. housing that costs at least 20% less than the market rate. Moreover, market prices and market rents are so high that even "affordable housing" is beyond the reach of people on lower or even average incomes.

A major share of the athletes' village was sold off to the investment arm of the Qatari ruling family*. The building of public housing has lagged terribly in Britain in the last 30 years yet here we see housing built with public money sold to foreign billionaires. It makes people wonder who the Olympics was for.

London 2012 also set itself the ambitious goal of getting more young people to participate in sport. The slogan of the games was: "Inspire a Generation". I see this as a worthy aim. There is a worrying trend towards obesity* in the UK bringing numerous health problems. But unfortunately the goal does not appear to have been achieved. Surveys indicate that there was a spike in sports participation in 2012 but it has declined since.

The Olympics was intended to be a "one-off* corrective"* that would generate huge interest in sport based on the theory that young people are inspired by seeing top athletes. But it seems this may be "just a theory"— and one that cannot replace a co-ordinated national policy. There has been a long-term problem of UK schools selling off their playing fields for development. And while there are now excellent new "legacy" sports facilities in London, important venues* such as Sheffield's main athletics stadium and Newcastle's City Pool have closed since 2012.

East London is traditionally a poorer area of the capital and it has been regenerated by the Olympics. But London as a whole and the South East of England is the richest region in the UK, so it is arguably unfair that the whole nation paid to develop a part of the capital while more deprived regions had no such boost.

As with the Olympic Stadium, the overall cost of the games ballooned*. The final budget *tripled* to £9.3 billion from the initial estimate in 2005. This happened despite the financial crisis and huge recession that happened in between. Some people argued that we should *reduce* expenditure and host an "austerity games" because of the recession but such arguments were given short shrift. The UK was apparently obliged to deliver on its promises to the International Olympic Committee, made during the bid.

Then, during the Olympics, IOC officials were permitted to use special "Olympic lanes" to whizz* through the London traffic, while citizens of London were confined* to the crowded, remaining portion of the road. The British will generally put up with inconvenience as long as everyone else shares it but they detest just this sort of "queue-jumping".

The most damaging thing of all, in my view, was the claim made after the Olympics that the games had been delivered on budget. (They even made a show of "returning" a small portion of the unused budget.) This is only true if you forget that the budget was tripled. It reminded me of George Orwell's novel *1984*, in which citizens were obliged to rejoice* that the chocolate rations* had been increased when they knew very well they used to get more before. The "on budget games" is a political lie that seems to assume the public is stupid and can be made to accept what it is told. That alone is enough to make 2012 a bitter memory for me.

Chapter
14

Keeping It Brief

When I lived in Japan I came to enjoy the way people abbreviate* words. I liked *Mon-Naka* (Monzen Nakacho) and *Shimo-Kita* (Shimo-Kitazawa). I liked the ones derived from English, such as *rajikase* (from "radio" and "cassette") and *famiresu* ("family restaurant"). It took me a bit longer to understand how *Nikkei* meant "Japan economics" but at least that was more logical than Osaka University being shortened to *Handai*. I still don't think it makes sense that the *Meishin* expressway is short for "Nagoya and Kobe".

It got me thinking about the way we abbreviate in English and I realised it's less logical than I assumed. I thought that we mostly just cut off the end of words to make a shorter version and, indeed, that is often the case. We say "wellies" to mean "Wellington boots", "gym" for "gymnasium" and "telly" for "television". (In all of those examples, the shorter word is far more commonly used than the full word.)

But we also sometimes instead cut off the *start* of the word. An obvious example would be "phone" for "telephone". It seems strange as the phone was invented before the television, so it wasn't the case that the abbreviation "telly" was already taken.

Then there are words where we use a sound from the middle, such as "fridge" to mean "refrigerator". This isn't at all intuitive* and I can remember as a boy being confused when someone said "refrigerator". I knew "fridge" but couldn't guess they were the same thing.

It seems that people naturally tend to make short words end in -y or -ie, like telly and wellies. Other examples end up quite far from the original word. In the north of England people sometimes say "leccy" for "electricity" while in the south some people say "sarnie" for "sandwich". "brolly" to mean "umbrella" is common all over England.

Whole words can be dispensed with*. A "cuppa" means a "cup of tea". (I don't think it is ever used to mean coffee or any other drink.) If someone asks if you "fancy a pint?" they mean "a pint of beer" (or possibly cider). It cannot mean a pint of milk, though we also buy milk in pints.

Football (or "footie") seems to have a lot of abbreviations. A referee is usually a "ref", a substitute is a "sub" and the goalkeeper is the "goalie". "Keepie uppies" is the skill in which you juggle* the ball without letting it hit the ground. Many teams have a shorter version of their names: "Spurs" and "Man U" refer to Tottenham Hotspur and Manchester United. "Pool" is for Blackpool and "Pools" is for Hartlepool United.

The city of Birmingham is sometimes called "Brum" and its people are "Brummies".

This abbreviation derives from the old name of the city (Bromwicham).

There are abbreviated versions for the various counties* of England. Bedfordshire is *Beds* and Lincolnshire is *Lincs* (logically enough) but Hampshire is *Hants* and Northamptonshire is *Nhants*. Oxon is short for Oxford University, derived from its Latin name *Oxoniensis*. So my degree is BA (Oxon). Cambridge University is *Cantabrigiensis*, which is shortened to *Cantab*. Oxford students jokingly call Cambridge students "tabs".

Almost all personal names have shorter versions; some have several. Richard, for example, could be Rich, Richie, Rick, Ricky, Dick or Dickie.

Americans find some British abbreviations funny such as when we say "brill" to mean "brilliant" or "fab" to mean "fabulous" (there is a famous British TV programme called *Ab Fab*, short for "absolutely fabulous"). On the other hand, when we want to emphasise something the English sometimes deliberately lengthen words, such as saying "super-duper" instead of just "super".

Obviously we use initials sometimes for brevity*. MP means "member of parliament" and DJ, or deejay, means "disk jockey". BA is "bachelor of arts". People often write PBAB to mean "please bring a bottle" to a party. I like TTFN, which means "ta-ta for now"* (i.e. "see you soon") because the short version is so close to the original you can almost hear it.

However, in English we *don't* say CM to mean "commercial" or NG to mean "no good". The term ATM is in use but more English people say "cash machine" instead.

I wonder how many Japanese people know that we say PJs to mean "pyjamas"? (We also say "jim-jams" for "pyjamas", though this isn't really an abbreviation.)

So in English we abbreviate a lot in various ways. For a long time, though, I thought there was no equivalent of the Japanese way of combining two abbreviated words (such as *rajikase*, or *rimokon* from "remote" and "control"). Then recently I was at the supermarket and found a pie made with banana and toffee, or Banoffee Pie as it's called.

Chapter **15**

The Japan I Didn't Like

I quite often get asked why I left Japan when, clearly, it is a country that I really like. I find it difficult to explain because there is more than one reason and it was quite a difficult decision. So sometimes I simply answer: "I got tired of bumping* my head."

People don't know how to react to that answer because they aren't sure if I am joking. Of course, that wasn't "the reason" I left Japan and the answer is rather flippant*. But it is also partially true. I like Japan, Japanese people and Japanese culture. Overall, I enjoyed my life in Japan but it was a fact that I experienced some issues that rather irritated me.

I don't know if you have ever banged your head but it really, really hurts. I banged my head a lot in Japan. Once I banged my head so hard I nearly passed out. Another time I hit my head and it bled for 20 minutes. During one maddening* week, I banged my head three times. I am tall but not incredibly tall (about 190 centimetres). I have met Japanese people who are as tall as me, or taller. Is it really reasonable to continue to make low doorways that cause a significant number of people to experience injury?

I find it difficult to work when it is noisy. When I am writing I put on music to cover any sound from outside (right now, I am listening to Bach's Cello Suite No. 1). But when I was in Tokyo, this wasn't enough. I would frequently be distracted by the horrible noise pollution of trucks collecting "large-scale rubbish". They seemed to circle the neighbourhood for hours. Even worse is election time, when arrogant people noisily shout their names from cars all day for weeks on end. Is that really the best way to win votes?

I used to go to the gym to exercise and

de-stress. I used to run on the machines and work up a tremendous sweat. My clothes would be soaking wet and for years I assumed I was a freakishly sweaty person. But when I went to the gym in America or England, bizarrely, I found I didn't sweat so much. Eventually I realised that the heating is just too strong in Japanese gyms (almost without exception). Japanese train carriages are also too hot in the cooler months but it was the gym that most annoyed me. It's a place to do exercise; exercise makes you hot; gyms don't need to be heated so much.

Japanese people are the most polite I have ever met. In more than ten years in Japan I had very few experiences of rudeness. But there is an exception. People, from friends to strangers, will blithely* say to you: "Wow, you are really sweating!" Of course, that is rude. You wouldn't say to someone that they are "a bit smelly" or say that their hair is quite greasy today. Yet people will point out that I am sweating when it is 33 degrees and humid, or when I have just left the public baths, or when I have finished at the gym. People know when they are sweating. There is no way to turn off the sweat, so there is no benefit to being told you are sweating. It only makes a person self-conscious to be told.

I like to ramble*. Sometimes, I would walk around town until I was lost and I would have to ask directions. Usually, people were very helpful but around one time in ten I would meet someone who couldn't tell me where the nearest station was, or which was the way to the river… I don't mind at all if someone says "I don't know" but sometimes the person wouldn't answer at all. He would tilt his head, he would suck in breath, pretend to be thinking or he might start a sentence and just stop in the middle ("This road is….") Obviously, if someone can't help, I just want to move on and ask someone else. But I felt obliged to wait for some sort of reply. Instead, I would be left hanging, waiting for an answer that wasn't coming. I experienced this kind of terrible communication skills in my work as a teacher and a reporter as well as in my everyday life.

Very rarely, but often enough to get under my skin, someone would act like they knew better than me about Japan simply by virtue of being Japanese. Like the time I was chatting with a man about drinking cultures and was told that "we" Japanese don't drink whisky. Not "Few people of my acquaintance drink whisky" or "Shochu is far more popular" but bluntly "We drink shochu and sake, not whisky." That put a swift end to my "intriguing" story that the Japanese possibly drink more Scotch than the English (the Scottish are a different matter). What bothered me was the implication that he couldn't be wrong on this matter because he was Japanese.

But possibly the worst thing was that I wasn't really allowed to criticise Japan when I lived there. If I wrote anything negative,

I was accused of "bashing"* Japan. Or if I complained about some aspect of Tokyo life, people would be upset or sometimes angry. I once made a Japanese girlfriend cry when I complained about some troublesome business with the ward office*. It seems that if I, as a foreigner, said anything bad about Japan people assumed that I hated Japan. The reality was very different. I thought it was great living in Japan but it's basically impossible to live somewhere and never find *anything* to dislike. I think it's reasonable for people to air their grievances* now and again. (It might even lead to some changes for the better.)

Think about it. If I really didn't like Japan, I wouldn't have stayed so long. Especially considering how often I banged my head.

Chapter 16

Perplexities of British Life

There are certain problems and situations that arise in the UK that seem particular to the British way of life. Some of them might occur in Japan or other countries, to a greater or lesser extent. But to me, they are "typical" of my life in England and not something I experienced much when I lived in Tokyo.

The profusion* of apples

Many English people have gardens and quite often these have apple trees. I have a single apple tree and every year it produces *hundreds* of apples. Dozens will fall from the tree on a windy day in season. They get bruised*, usually have a wormhole or two, are often a bit blemished* or may be not fully ripe*. But I cannot throw them away as they are *my apples*, that *I* grew in my garden. Right now, I have about 50 apples in my fridge while my freezer is also full of Tupperware containers of apples that I cooked (with a bit of sugar and some blackberries). It's more than I can eat. Yet it's hard to even give the apples away because most people just prefer to buy perfect apples from the shops. Or someone else struggling with their crop may have already given them a big bagful of apples.

Barrels of beer*

At some stage in his life—maybe as a student, maybe in retirement—the typical Englishman will decide to make his own beer. Usually he makes this from a home-brewing kit which is said to be "foolproof"*. The problem is that the kits produce beer that is not bad, but not as good as "proper beer". And suddenly there is 40 pints of it to be consumed within a couple of weeks. So the man will invite his friends round and they will be obliged to drink several pints of this not-very-good beer which they must praise, while knowing it will probably give them a nasty hangover* the next day. (I have been both the victim and the host of such parties.)

Embarrassing collection day

In my town, the rubbish is collected weekly but "cans and bottles" are collected bi-weekly. This is always a sobering* moment because I can see how many empty wine bottles and beer cans I have generated in just 14 days. Indeed, the plastic container gets so heavy that it is a nuisance to carry from the kitchen to outside the house. It's embarrassing so I sneak* the heavy container out late at night when none of my neighbours see me, even though several of them have the same issue. Other people try to get round* the problem by putting a few empty cans into the regular rubbish bag or bringing a few empty bottles to the bins at the supermarket when they go shopping.

The rain-or-shine dilemma

The British weather is unpredictable and there is a cliché that we can experience "four seasons in one day". Quite often, just as I am leaving the house, I have to stop for a few minutes while I decide whether to put on sunscreen or whether to pack an umbrella. You might think it's simple: umbrella if it's raining, sunscreen if it's hot. But it's not so straightforward. You might put on the sunscreen only for it to cloud over ten minutes later and for it to rain the rest of the day. Or vice versa*. But it's even more complicated than that. There are days when you will need both… and days when you bring both but need neither.

Remote clutter*

This happens in other countries too, but the experience of having too many remote controls is widespread in Britain. Today, people not only have DVD players and TVs but have some sort of "box" from Sky or Virgin or some such through which they watch TV programmes. Almost no two households have the same set up so when you are at someone else's house it's nearly impossible to navigate their TV, unless you are quite techie*. Personally, I even manage to forget how my own system works if I am away for a couple of weeks. Today, I tried to pause a live television programme and ended up starting the DVD player. Wrong remote!

Two hands, five drinks

The English buy "rounds" of beers. That is, we take turns to buy drinks at the pub for our friends. It's a nice, reciprocal* custom and part of it is that the buyer will go and queue at the bar for the drinks while his friends relax and chat. Many Englishmen are good at carrying numerous drinks, gripping bottles with their arms while holding several glasses with their fingers and manoeuvring* their way through a crowded pub. But if I ever had this skill, I forgot it during my time in Tokyo.

Card confusion

Most English people have somewhere between two and five bank cards. I have eight. Some are "contactless" (you just tap them on the payment device, conveniently), some have "chip and PIN", some are credit cards and some debit cards. Each card should have a different PIN (secret number). Some cards are for emergency use only, some give "cashback" points, some have a limit for usage each month. On top of this, most supermarkets have "loyalty cards", which you swipe* to collect points to spend in the store. So this makes for wallets full of plastic cards and a bewildering* choice of which card to use when. I frequently use the wrong card in the wrong shop, enter the PIN from a different card, try to tap cards that require to be inserted and so on.

Train nightmares

I am not a trainspotter* but I literally dream of trains. We have an incredibly complicated train system, with various different train companies and dozens of different types of ticket. There is a huge price difference between doing it the cheapest way (book online, choose a specific off-peak train, get code number, put the code into a machine at the station to retrieve* ticket) and the most expensive (just turn up at the station and buy a ticket for the next train). You get fined for having the wrong ticket, which is easy to do because of the complicated system. You can be forced to buy a new ticket (as I was once) if you buy online but don't bring the credit card with which you purchased the ticket. Most English people find it annoying but accept it as part of life. But I remember how easy it all was in Japan, so the stress of English trains invades my dreams.

Chapter
17

A Journey into Japanese

There's a little joke that I like to play on English friends. I tell them that I have a method to teach them a basic vocabulary of a hundred Japanese words *in less than ten minutes*. Usually, they are a bit sceptical* but then I begin: telephone card, shampoo, carpet, helicopter, rugby, internet...

I remember one friend joked back that I had chosen an easy language to learn if Japanese consists entirely of slightly mispronounced English. Of course, "loan words" from foreign languages form only a small part of Japanese. But also it's not so "easy" to master loan words because many of them come from languages other than English and even the English ones can be far from the original in meaning, usage or pronunciation.

In fact, loan words are a fascinating aspect of Japanese in which you can see the flexibility of the language and the creativity of its speakers. Loan words exist in great variety, from the mundane* to the hilarious, from the simple to the complex.

There are a few loan words that are buried so far back in history that even Japanese people don't always know their origin. It seems that the word *sebiro* (though usually written in kanji not katakana) derives from Savile Row, the street in London famous for its tailoring. I can just imagine a Meiji Era Englishman showing off his suit and saying, "It's Savile Row, you know!" and a Japanese person deducing* that "Savile Row" must be the name for this strange mode of clothing.

Similarly, there is a story that when Westerners brought pet dogs to Japan, the Japanese began to call these *kameya* because their owners were always shouting "Come here!" to them. It's a shame* this word fell into disuse* because I think it would be handy to have a word specifically to mean a pet dog.

For a long time, I assumed that many loan words were just "mispronounced" English. Words like *kokku* (cook), *arerugii* (allergy) and *botan* (button) were recognisable but quite different from English. I eventually realised that they were in fact taken from other languages, such as Dutch, German and Portuguese, so the word might be close to the English but not the same.

It was even longer before I spotted that the word beer in Japanese could be *biiru* (from Dutch) or *bia* (as in *bia gāden*, from English).

Compound words interest me and I was intrigued* to note that sometimes Japanese create new words by adding loan words to Japanese, such as *shabon-dama* (soap bubble, using Spanish + Japanese) and *man-tan* (full tank, Japanese + English). My favourite is *nominikeishon*, made from the Japanese *nomu*, to drink, and the latter half of the English word "communication". So "having some drinks to enable people to open up a bit with each other, particularly co-workers". ("*nominikeishon*" is a much snappier way to say it.)

Quite often, loan words in Japanese have changed their meaning. "Cunning" is an adjective in English meaning crafty* (clever in a bad way). In Japanese *kanningu suru* is a verb meaning "to cheat in an exam". I can see how that one came about, but others are stranger. I wonder who first came up with the idea that a bride walking up the aisle is walking the *bājin rōdo* ("virgin road"). Clearly this is an example of "Made-in-Japan English".

A very strange one is *furaingu stāto*. In English a "flying start" is an excellent start, something which will get you ahead of others. There are companies called Flying Start and courses that offer you "a flying start". But in Japanese it means a false or illegal start, something which will get you disqualified or at least called back to the starting line.

I lived in Japan for a long time and it influenced me in many ways. That included me picking up some Japanese-English that, it transpires, isn't correct English. I thought "plus alpha" (*purasu arufa*) meant "a little something extra" because that is the way I had heard it used in Japan for years. English speakers didn't understand me. Once I even wrote a story for a newspaper about a "busjack" incident. (The editors corrected it to "bus hijacking".) I had to wean myself off* saying that something is "my boom" at the moment, as I noticed English people thought I was odd.

Weirdly, some Japanese-English has actually found its way back into English. A "salaryman" specifically means a Japanese company employee (with connotations of loyalty to the company and long working hours). There is also a dish called "curry rice", to mean Japanese-style mild curry on sticky Japanese rice.

Most foreigners in Japan have some favourite loan words. I like *gattsu pōzu* ("guts pose", when a sportsman poses dramatically for the cameras or crowd); it's an evocative expression using English words, but isn't used in English. I am amused by *herusu mētā* ("health meter", to mean weighing scales); it's actually become *more* apt* in an era when some scales measure body fat and can calculate BMI. But my favourite is probably *pēpā doraibā* ("paper driver", for someone who has a license but doesn't actually drive a car); an economical way of expressing a common phenomenon.

Occasionally I had some unfortunate experiences as a result of loan words. Once, on a hot summer day, I came across a canned drink called *saidā*, which I assumed was going to be apple cider. Imagine my disappointment when it turned out it should rather be called "soda". Years later, I heard the expression *defure supairaru*. Somehow I misheard it and for a while I opined* about the "deathly spiral" in which the Japanese economy was trapped. (I still think it sounds closer to "deathly" than "deflationary spiral".)

I always kept my ears open for loan words but even so there are a couple I have only learned recently. Until a friend used the word a couple of months ago, I didn't know that those thin summer blankets made from towelling are called *taoruketto*. I knew the word *ēru* meant "to cheer on" but only recently found out that it comes from the English "yell" (which is more normally associated with angry people shouting than sports fans cheering).

While writing this, I did a bit of reading about Japanese loan words and found a "mistake". I read on one website that *ryukkusakku* was from German, whereas I was sure "rucksack" was an English word. Of course, when I thought about the sound and look of that word I realised that it was adopted into English from German. So now I am wondering if I can learn a hundred words of German in ten minutes.

Chapter
18

"Sort of" Equivalents

Comparing Japan to Britain can be a bit like comparing "chalk and cheese", to use the English expression. In other words, it's very difficult because even when things seem alike they can be very different, just as chalk in its natural state* resembles certain types of crumbly* white cheese... but shouldn't be put in your mouth.

And yet, sometimes I come across things that are different but occupy a similar "cultural space" in their respective countries. This all may sound a bit odd but here are a few things that I found in Japan that have a "sort-of-equivalent" in Britain.

Tsubasa Ōzora, the footballing hero of the Japanese comic series *Captain Tsubasa*, has a counterpart in **Roy Race**, hero of the English comic series *Roy of the Rovers*. Unlike Tsubasa,

Roy is an adult and a professional footballer from the start but other aspects of the story are similar. Roy is handsome, brave and brilliant at football. He is also an "ideal Englishman" who is honest and decent* on or off the pitch. English kids (including me) dreamed of being like him: playing on boldly* even if injured and leading the team to an incredible victory against great odds*.

The Japanese word *sento* is "public bath" in English but England no longer has bath houses (though they used to exist). The nearest *cultural* equivalent of the *sento* is perhaps the "public house", or "**pub**" as we call it. People gather here for relaxation, to meet other local people and chat for a bit. Some people go occasionally, some go regularly on the way back from work. Japanese don't go to the *sento* just to wash (they could do that at home, usually) and British people don't go to the pub just to drink alcohol (they could do that at home). They go for a change of scene and a bit of interaction*.

Foreigners who live in Japan are very likely to be asked at some stage if they like **natto**. Indeed, they may well be offered natto to taste. Japanese people seem to think that foreigners will be repulsed by* the very sight of natto and disgusted by its taste and sticky texture. They may be right. We don't have natto in England but we do have **Marmite**. Marmite is a sticky, black paste made from yeast extract*. You spread it on toast. It has a tangy, salty taste that a lot of people dislike. Children are more likely to hate it than adults but a lot of British adults won't touch it* either. And the British are also very curious about making foreigners try it. We think it's an amusing and uniquely British food and wonder whether only we can tolerate it.

Japan has some pretty lively festivals like **Onbashira**, where people ride logs down a hill, or the **Hadaka Matsuri** where (nearly) naked men compete in teams to get hold of amulets* thrown into the crowd. For a long time, I thought these kinds of events were uniquely Japanese but when I went back to England I found there are "somewhat similar" festivals in parts of Britain that I had never visited. In Gloucester, there is a **Cheese Rolling** event, where a huge round cheese is sent hurtling* down a steep hill and people race down the hill to catch it. It's pretty dangerous and people get hurt but it's also very popular. In Derbyshire, the people of two towns compete to carry a ball across several miles in the **Royal Shrovetide Football Match**. It's played intensely* and is quite physical, with lots of jostling* but not open violence. It's played for fun, prestige and bonding*.

One of Japan's most important cultural figures is **Doraemon**, the robot cat from the future. Everyone knows him, everyone loves him and everyone wishes they had their own real-life Doraemon as a friend. In Britain, people of my age wish they could have their own

Bagpuss, a sleepy, magical cat with pink and white fur. Bagpuss belonged to Emily but he spent most of his time (when not asleep) with other dolls and "animals" that only he could bring to life. Together, they fixed broken things, sang songs and told stories (on a short and wonderful television programme).

Japan's national sport is **sumo**. In England, the nation's favourite sport is football (and we claim to have invented it) but football now belongs to the world. However, we still have **cricket**. A game of cricket can feel rather slow because the moments of action tend to occur at quite long intervals. It's more interesting to watch the highlights than watch in real time. A lot of the sport is quite technical and can only be fully appreciated by people who understand the various strokes (with the bat) and types of ball (bowled by the bowler). It may be an English sport but foreigners seem to be better at it than us (Australians, Pakistanis et al*). It may be a bit of a stretch*, but I see similarities between sumo and cricket.

Botchan is my favourite Japanese novel. It was the first one I bought when I went to Japan and the only one I have read more than twice. It's a compact, comical, well-written story of a young man struggling to adapt to life as an adult working in a school in a period when the world is changing. Later, I read Kingsley Amis' novel **Lucky Jim** and I kept recalling the story of Botchan. *Lucky Jim* is a short but brilliant comic classic about Jim, a young, accident-prone teacher thrown into a tricky situation in his first university post in post-war Britain. We sympathise with Jim (just as with Botchan) even as he makes a mess of his situation, partly because he is out of his home environment and surrounded by people he doesn't like (just as with Botchan). Neither care for their jobs.

So Japan and Britain may not be quite "chalk and cheese" after all. Cheese and tofu, perhaps?

Chapter
19

Help! I Am Turning into a Trainspotter

In Britain, there is no hobby more embarrassing than trainspotting. There is a dismissive* nickname—"anoraks"—for people who love trains. It's because anorak coats are considered practical but unfashionable and trainspotters always seem to be wearing them. They also seem to always have a flask* for hot drinks (or soup maybe), though trainspotters are never called "flasks". When I first went to university, some of the older students organised a Trainspotters' Club, which they encouraged us to join. It was a big joke: there was no club and the aim was to catch out all the "uncool" new boys foolish enough to sign up*.

So, here's my problem: travelling in Japan has turned me into a big train fan. I wouldn't call myself a trainspotter. After all, I don't hang out at stations taking notes on engine types or recording the sounds of various trains. (And I don't own an anorak.) But I have developed an affection for* train travel that could be mistaken for a mania. When British friends ask me about Japan, I often find myself singing the praises* of the country's trains. I try to explain how great it is to be in a country with such reliable trains but usually people's eyes begin to glaze over*. Sometimes they respond, "Oh yes, I've heard of the bullet train" and I find myself explaining that it's so much *more* than that.

I don't think I would be so in love with trains were I from Germany or the Netherlands or any country with a decent train system. The problem with Britain is that it used to lead the world in trains (we actually invented them) but somewhere in the last few decades we lost the way terribly. It happened in my lifetime so we can sense what it would be like to have a functioning and extensive train network but we can't experience it in Britain anymore. It's frustrating beyond words. So when I travel in Japan it's like a burden has been lifted from me. Just turning up at the station and finding all the trains are running is something I take for granted in Japan but something we all have to worry about in Britain.

I could write a book about my bad experiences on trains in the UK (though it would be the most boring book ever written). Trains get cancelled when it is cold, when it is hot, when there are "leaves on the track" (these words cause British train commuters to shake with rage), for "essential maintenance" or even for no discernible* reason. Personally, I am most infuriated* at the way the whole network shuts down over the holidays, i.e. just when people are most likely to want to travel to visit relatives. For example, the trains to London from Colchester (where I live) stopped on the evening of the 23rd of December, ahead of Christmas 2016, and didn't resume until January 3rd in the new year. Ten days without the option to get into London at a time when many of my friends would be free to go for drinks!

As it happens, I can report that fact without my blood pressure shooting up ten points because I wasn't in England this Christmas. I spent the winter holiday travelling in Japan. Christmas Day I rode trains to Himeji. From there I went to Kobe, Nara and Kyoto (with excursions to Arima, Fushimi Inari and a visit to some old friends near Kakogawa) before returning to Tokyo. I rode dozens of trains at all times of day, run by various train companies and never once had a negative experience worth mentioning. The trains were quite crowded at times but to me that just shows they are the first choice of transport for millions of people because they are reliable and cheap. (If I were to think of a slogan for British trains it would be "Unreliable and

Expensive!")

I have a particular affection for Hankyu railways. The Hankyu line (Rokko station in Kobe) was nearest to me when I first lived in Japan. The trains to Sannomiya and Umeda (Osaka) were so regular and fast. I could go to Kyoto and back on a day trip for just over a thousand yen. I still love the maroon* colour of the trains; somehow the carriages are reminiscent of* the great romantic era of train travel. Walking a little further from where I lived down towards the sea there was the JR station and a bit further still was the Hanshin line, from where I would get the train to Koshien Stadium now and then. There was a choice of train companies, competition and convenience. Trains in Japan gave me freedom to travel and enhanced* my life.

It's not that I don't love the Shinkansen—it is a sleek*, wonderful mode of transport—but rather that I think it overshadows* how great the rest of the train system is. I love, for example, how you can get on one train and it runs for a long distance across lines owned by two or three different train companies without the need to change trains and without incurring* much higher fares. For example, I got on a Hanshin train in Kobe and got off the same train at a Kintetsu station in Nara. The level of cooperation and coordination is extraordinary. By contrast, I once tried to travel from Lancaster to the Lake District in England. I had about 13 minutes to change trains at Penrith station but the Virgin train I first boarded stopped en route for 15 minutes (for no apparent reason). When I got to the interchange station, the other company's train had left exactly on time, not waiting the couple of minutes for the connecting train. (The next train wasn't leaving for another hour.)

This time in Japan I made the strange decision to use JR's super-cheap, local-trains-only "Seishun 18 kippu" since I was travelling during the holiday period when you can use them, since I figured the Shinkansen would be crowded, and because I was curious to do something I last did as a student more than twenty years ago. I have to say it was great. I stared out the window* (Mt Fuji!), studied a bit, did some work, ate a "bento", slept for a while and even watched a DVD on my computer until the battery ran out. The time flew by once I accepted that it wasn't going to be a quick journey.

I had checked the timetable and it said if I left at 09.30 from Kyoto I would get to the station nearest to my friend's house in Kawasaki at 18.09, using seven trains over 506 km (at a cost to me of 2,370 yen). When I finally arrived I noticed it was *exactly* 18.09. I was so happy and impressed that I wanted someone to take my photo under the clock on the platform. But then I realised that such a photo would mark me forever as a trainspotter.

Chapter **20**

Best of British Manners

Japanese are famous for their good manners and on the whole I think it is fair to say that the Japanese are more polite than the British. I like the way, for example, Japanese people are wary of* walking across someone's line of vision. They will try to avoid doing so and, if they must do it, will hurry past holding up a hand of apology. I also like the way, at a restaurant, when some food arrives with a slice of lemon, a Japanese person will first ask fellow diners if it's okay to put lemon juice on and then will squeeze the lemon with one hand while using the other hand to block any lemon juice from spraying over other people. These are just a couple of examples of considerate manners that I see in Japan and not in Britain.

But there are also some habits that I appreciate when I am in the UK or miss when I am in Japan. Prominent* among these is the manners of drivers towards pedestrians. We have a lot of so-called zebra crossings in Britain and you need only approach one on foot for cars to stop to allow you to cross the road. Sometimes it is already too late for a driver to stop at the crossing when he sees you and he will instead wave in apology, even though the next car is sure to stop and you will only have to wait a few seconds at most. But it's different in Japan, where cars will usually only stop if there is also a red light commanding them to do so. Occasionally a kind driver will stop, but in Tokyo I usually had to wait until there was a break in the traffic. And that made me wonder what is the point of the zebra crossing. If I was just anyway waiting for a time when there are no cars coming, I don't need a zebra crossing.

The British are also quite "generous" when it doesn't cost them anything. I happen to live in front of a big car park and almost every day I see people giving away parking tickets. People usually buy a four-hour ticket but often only need to park for an hour or so. As they leave, people will offer the ticket with three hours remaining to others who are just arriving. Sometimes I see people running over to the ticket machines to stop others from buying a new ticket. British people will also do this with train tickets. There are some tickets that can be used all day and when someone has finished with their ticket they will deliberately leave it where it can easily be found by others who might want it. Strictly speaking, it is not allowed to "transfer" tickets this way but in Britain this is everyday behaviour and it seems you can't stop people doing it.

It is said that the British have a talent for queueing. "An Englishman, even when he is alone, will form an orderly queue of one," as one comedian once said. There does seem to be a strong sense of fair play in British queueing.

The British will, for example, usually form a single queue when possible. You don't see it so much these days but if, say, there were two public telephones British people would typically wait in one queue in the order of arrival and go to whichever became available first. That is the fairest system but in a lot of countries people would form two queues. Another example of queuing manners is seen at the supermarket. When someone has a lot of shopping he might look at the person *behind* him in the queue and let him go first if he has only two or three items. The person in front has the right to be served first but will altruistically* wait an extra one minute to save another person a wait of three minutes.

There is one way in which Japanese pedestrians are worse than British pedestrians: a significant number of Japanese have a bad habit of walking with their faces turned down. This used to mainly be a problem when it rains and some people pull their umbrellas down below their eye level and walk looking downwards. But nowadays the problem is worse because of the growing use of "smart phones" and other hand-held devices. Quite often when I am walking in Japan I have to swerve* around someone who is obliviously walking straight towards me staring at a screen. I can't say this never happens in Britain, but it is far rarer than in Japan. I want to scold Japanese people for doing this but instead just sing a line from the classic song by Kyu Sakamoto ("ue o muite, arukou"). Unfortunately, this doesn't seem to work because the kind of self-absorbed person who would walk around staring at a screen is not the kind of person to notice a subtle hint in the words of a song.

The Japanese and British have it in common that they will apologise if you bump into them. It seems to be instinctive* to people in both countries to say sorry even when it is not their fault. (In other countries, people are more likely to say "be careful" in admonishment*.)

But the British seem to take apologizing one step further. People will say, for example, "Sorry but you are stepping on my foot." I sometimes thought this is ridiculous but then recently a man at a pub—accidentally but carelessly—picked up my beer and took a sip* from it. I heard myself say, "Sorry but I think that's mine", and I realised I am British too.

Chapter
21

Japanglophilia Cafe

Years ago when I was living in New York, a friend told me there was a Peruvian-Chinese restaurant in my neighbourhood and asked me if I wanted to go. Intrigued, I agreed immediately. I wondered what on earth *Peruvian-Chinese* could be. When we got there it was an unusually large place and I assumed that it must be two restaurants in a single premises: Chinese food at the back, Peruvian at the front. But no; it really was a fusion restaurant serving Chinese food with a Peruvian influence or vice-versa.

For ages afterwards I would try and think of a more unusual combination and would joke to my friend that tonight I fancied* Lebanese-Ghanaian or ask her if she could recommend a good French-Nepalese place.

By now you may have guessed that I am thinking of a new style of food appropriate to the theme of this book. I want to create an imaginary Japanese-English fusion restaurant.

Firstly, I thought it couldn't be haute cuisine. It should be a fairly down-to-earth* place because I can't think how to blend high-end sushi with "posh" English dishes like beef Wellington. But I could—just about—think of ideas for putting more common foods together.

The restaurant would have to be in a big cosmopolitan city where there are a lot of people willing to try something unusual. It should be somewhere Japanese food is quite common, where people might say "I ate Japanese a lot recently so I'd rather not have straight Japanese again." I guess that would mean a fashionable area of London or maybe Brooklyn in New York.

My place would serve a cheap breakfast to appeal to early rising, health-conscious people but also to clubbers* on the way home from a big night out. Porridge-with-a-Japanese-twist and green tea would be the "morning set". The "twist" in the porridge would vary from time to time but would be something that you see in Japan but not the UK: ginkgo nuts*, goji berries*, flakes of nori, dried natto etc. In autumn, I would put chunks of persimmon* in. But I wouldn't call them persimmons, I would call them "kaki" so that people would think they are getting some rare, exotic fruit that has been flown in overnight from Wakayama.

By late morning, the kitchen would be fully opened and instead of the traditional English fried breakfast we would start serving a cooked brunch of "*Wafu* bubble and squeak". Bubble and squeak is an old English dish made by frying vegetables in potatoes. Typically, these are vegetables left over* from a roast dinner, so cabbage, carrots, peas and sprouts*. It is not exactly healthy but it is nutritional and hearty* (as well as thrifty*). Personally, I never liked bubble and squeak because I don't like the vegetables used. At my restaurant, we would use Japanese vegetables such as *gobo*, *kogomi* and *komatsuna*. The potatoes would just be regular potatoes but if you wanted to add flavour we would offer Bull-Dog Sauce from Japan (since this is actually derived from the British invention Worcestershire sauce it is perfect for this restaurant).

Our lunchtime fish and chips would be "tempura fish and chips". The fish would be served in smaller pieces than traditional English and lightly sprinkled* with malt vinegar and "*shio-kosho* salt and pepper". The chips would be "lotus root *renkon* chips" ("a healthy, Eastern alternative to the starchy* British chip", the menu would explain). We would serve okra instead of mushy peas*, the traditional side dish. Okra isn't strictly Japanese but the waiters would explain that it is a popular vegetable in Japan, if asked. Under no circumstances would we mention that another name for okra is "lady's fingers", just because the manager (me!) finds that name weird and unsettling*.

Famously, fish and chip shops in Scotland sometimes serve deep-fried Mars bars*. (It is quite rare, I should add.) Of course, this cannot be healthy but I have heard that it is a fascinating culinary* experience and I think it might be okay in small quantities as a very occasional treat. I would get my chef to experiment with deep-fried Pocky as a dessert.

The beauty of *okonomiyaki* is that you can put almost anything into it. It's a sort of Japanese equivalent of bubble and squeak. So, just as my restaurant's bubble and squeak has Japanese ingredients, the *okonomiyaki* would have English ingredients such as slivers* of black pudding (a rich, blood sausage) or kippers* (smoked herring). I would have to get a chef from Western England as I have learned from living in Japan that chefs from the capital or eastern parts of a country cannot make good *okonomiyaki*. There would be no *beni-shoga*, as it tastes bad and looks artificial. Even if the restaurant fails, this will be my legacy: that I helped everyone notice that bright red shards* of sharp tasting ginger isn't a good thing to throw into food.

Our yakitori wouldn't be authentic. It would just be roast beef and roast lamb cut into bite-sized chunks and put on a skewer*. It would be dipped in gravy or mint sauce. This may seem pointless but people like food that is easy to eat and the yakitori format is convenient.

We would serve English beers (real ales only) but the snacks to go with them would be Japanese: edamame, *goya* chips and *saki ika*. Sake would be served cold with raw cashew nuts and English sea salt.

I spent a while thinking what to call my imaginary restaurant. Initially I was trying to find a good name invoking the idea that we were "sister nations" or "fellow island nations" (Two Sisters? Islands Cuisine?) Finally I hit on the perfect, accurate, honest name. I would call my restaurant Confusion.

Chapter 22

A Collection of Collectives

When I am showing off to my English friends, I tell them how terribly difficult it is to learn to count things in Japanese. I tell them that there are dozens of different ways to count and list a few of the main categories: big animals, small animals, people, thin things, books, fish, birds, sheets of paper and so on.

Then I tell them that there is a special way to count chopsticks which *even some young Japanese do not know*. And then, for my final flourish*, I tell them that rabbits are counted as if they were birds. My friends are amazed and tell me that I must be really clever to master such a complicated language.

As it happens, I didn't find the counting system the hardest part of learning Japanese and I also found it interesting to see how Japanese categorised things. It was a small insight into Japanese culture. Moreover, I don't think the counting system is proof that Japanese is uniquely difficult because in fact we have a similar and even more complicated concept in English: collective nouns.

I recommend that Japanese students of English should try to learn a few of these for two reasons. Firstly, it is a rare chance to be better than a native speaker. Very few English people are masters of collective nouns. Secondly, I think it is a rich and interesting aspect of our language.

To start with people: we usually refer to a "crowd" of people (if it's a lot) or a "group" (if it's a smaller number). A "mob" would imply that the people were angry or causing trouble. A "party" of people would not necessarily be having fun: it usually means they have a shared agenda.

We talk of a "pack" of wolves or dogs, implying that they work or hunt together. Curiously, we also say "a pack of cards" and "a pack of lies" (so we also use collective nouns for inanimate* objects and abstract concepts).

Creatures that come together for safety aren't called "packs". Sheep and birds both form a "flock" whereas cows and horses form a "herd". (If the horses are working in harness*, though, they are a "team".) We say a "school" of fish but a "pod" of whales or dolphins.

When people don't know what to say, they just try the general word "group". This doesn't sound too bad if the collective noun is obscure (giraffes, for example) but it sounds silly if someone says "a group of cows" because most people know it's a herd*. Recently, some people even say "bunch" for everything: a "bunch of animals" or a "bunch of elephants". I dislike this as the word makes me think instead of bananas and grapes.

I am not claiming to be an expert on collective nouns. There are some I had to look up before writing this: apparently it should be a "corps" of giraffes; and it turns out that it is correct to use "bunch" for deer (though "herd" is more common).

Some collective nouns are very evocative. We say a "pride" of lions, which is suitable for those magnificent animals. We say a "murder" of crows, which matches the sinister* appearance of those ugly birds. A "cloud" of gnats* is exactly what they look like when they get together and a "scourge" of mosquitoes is very apt. An "army" of ants is appropriate because they are so well organised, though I don't know why it is also an "army" of frogs.

Quite often, there is more than one collective term possible. For example, you can also say a "tower" of giraffes (which I think it funnier than "corps") or a "gam" of whales. Or the best term may vary depending on the situation: a "colony" of ants is better for describing them in their nest.

English people occasionally play a game testing each other's knowledge of the correct collective terms. The two I ask people are:

Gulp!

What is the term for vultures* feeding? And what do the Irish say for a large number of beers?

The answer to the first is a "wake" of vultures (a "wake" is normally used to mean a gathering of people before a funeral). The second is a "rake of pints", after the gardening tool that gathers up leaves. Both terms are memorable and funny (if darkly funny, in the first one).

Readers may know I have a special love of cormorants, so I want to end with one of my favourites. A group of cormorants together is, brilliantly, called a "gulp".

Chapter
23

The (Unexpected) Dividends of Thrift

We say that "a penny saved is a penny earned" but actually most English people are rather wasteful with money. When I lived in Japan, I picked up some useful thrifty habits by osmosis* and even wrote a story for an English newspaper about the amazing housekeeping tips of the Japanese. There were lots of books on the subject by housewives, I remember. But it was only a couple of years ago that I started to develop some thrift strategies. Some I gave up on, some I have kept up. Some I think are universal but some may be particular to me (and the place I live). The surprising thing was that I didn't just save money but gained a few interesting insights.

Don't buy it (if you don't need it)

This is a really obvious thing to do but the one that took me longest to adapt to. My particular weakness was for buying shirts, T-shirts and socks. I knew I didn't need any more clothes but would still occasionally "browse" the shops and then end up grabbing a "bargain". But I gradually managed to change my habits. Now, instead, I go back through my (ridiculously large) collection of clothes and dig out old purchases. Mostly they are in good condition as I rarely wore anything very often. In fact, I get more pleasure now from resurrecting* an old favourite than buying something new. Today, I am wearing a lovely T-shirt from the 2002 Korea-Japan World Cup. Very retro! (It prompted me to look up that it was on this day 15 years ago today that Japan drew 2-2 with Belgium; a game I remember well.)

Saving In my case, probably about £500 a year.

Worth it? Obviously it saves money to not

buy unneeded things. But it also helps you value the things you have.

Money falling from the sky

It rains often in England. In my garden I have a water butt, which is a big barrel that collects the rain from my roof. In summer, when it is dry, I use this to water the plants and grass in my garden but the other nine months of the year the garden doesn't need it and the water sits in the barrel. So, I decided to use that water to flush my toilets. Each morning, I go outside and refill 10 big plastic bottles from the butt. Six go in the downstairs toilet, four upstairs. It gets me out into the garden every day for a few minutes before I start work at my computer. Also, carrying the bottles up the stairs is a little bit of exercise, repeated daily. (I think of it as "being paid to exercise".) But most importantly, it's good for the environment. I live in one of the most densely populated and driest regions of Britain and we are all being asked to reduce water usage by 20 litres a day, which is almost exactly what I achieve by this.

Saving About £30 a year.

Worth it? No, not from a financial point of view. (But it does mean I don't mind so much when it rains...)

The supermarket trawl

I can visit three supermarkets in a 30-minute walk. I do that about four times a week, combining a walk with a break from work at about 6pm. This also happens to be the time when food near its "use-by" date tends to get reduced in price. I snap up bargains but am careful not to buy too much perishable food*. (I hate to throw food away.) Once a week I go to the market where I buy bagfuls of fruit and veg that will last me for a week (sometimes two) for just a few pound. So the cheapest food is also the healthiest.

Saving Hard to say precisely but definitely

more than £1,000 a year compared to an average person.

Worth it? Yes, if you have the time and a comparable situation.

Playing the banks at their own game*

You may be surprised that I owe several thousand pounds on credit cards. You will probably be astonished* to hear that the banks effectively pay me to do that. I got a credit card almost two years ago because there was a joining bonus (of £25). There was also no interest for the first 18 months. So when I made a big purchase, I paid with that credit card with the intention of paying off the money at the end of the 18 months. But when it came near, I found *another* bank would give me a credit card and almost three years no interest if I transferred my debt on to it from the old card. The point is to not use the credit card to borrow money you can't afford or buy things you don't need. It's to get the maximum amount of time to pay back for things you do have to buy. You have to keep to the rules and remember to pay it all back before the interest-free period ends. But, for example, I visited Japan twice in 2016 but won't have to finish paying for the tickets until early 2020. All the while, I have that money in a bank account paying me interest.

Saving About £100 a year in my case.

Worth it? As long as you do it right and aren't tempted to borrow money you wouldn't normally spend. (But the same offers wouldn't exist in Japan.)

Maximising gym membership

Most people join a gym and rarely go. I go to the gym a lot but sometimes don't even exercise. It's a bit strange but I often decide to go just for a shower. That means at the very least I have 1) gone for a walk and 2) saved a few pennies by using their hot water. But actually, most times when I go "just for a shower" I then decide to do half an hour's exercise or more. So, by being really mean with money, I sort of trick myself into doing some exercise. Also, there was the unexpected benefit of finding how rarely I have to clean the bath and shower in my house.

Savings £0 It's not a cash saving because the gym membership is more than the money saved in hot water. But it's better value for money to go 22 times a month, and exercise 18 times, than to go for exercise 10 times a month (for the same cost).

Worth it? Well, it helps keep my beer belly down a bit.

Some of my English friends laugh at my money-saving ways. They think it's miserly and say "money is for spending". I try to tell them about "opportunity cost"; I am not just saving money, I am choosing where and when to spend it. This evening, for example, I might treat myself to some lovely craft beers. But first I must grab a shower at the gym.

Chapter
24

The Juror Experience

If my life had worked out differently I would now be a civil servant*. In my final year at university I applied to work in the civil service and even passed its entrance exam. However, after I was summoned* for two days of interviews in London, I was rejected. I sometimes wonder what I did wrong and possibly it was that I strongly insisted in interview that there were no circumstances under which criminal trials* could be held without a jury*.

The interviewer cited the high cost of the system and suggested some trials didn't require juries. He mentioned that some trials last so long that getting twelve members of the public to serve was impractical*. He argued that certain types of crime, such as certain financial scams, were so complex that non-experts couldn't follow them and deliver a true verdict*. I rejected all his suggestions indignantly*. Whatever it may cost, however difficult it may be, however much effort must be expended educating the jurors, the jury system was a right (and duty) essential to our democratic system, I argued.

In retrospect*, I was being a bit obstinate. At least I could have acknowledged that juries might be waived* in trials involving organised crime, or other circumstances where intimidation* may be a problem. But at the time of the interview, I wouldn't accept that there was *any* alternative to juries.

I am recalling all this now because I have recently served as a juror for the first time. It was an interesting and educational process and I feel pleased that I did my duty, even though the timing was difficult for me and I lost some earnings as a result.

Instead of joining the civil service I went

to study in Japan. I remember being surprised and disturbed to hear at that time that there were no juries in Japanese trials. Of course, in 2009 Japan introduced a system of lay judges, which is akin to jury service, so I am guessing that few readers have yet been involved in a trial but that you may be one day.

The first thing people tell you about jury service is that "there's a lot of waiting around". That was especially true for me. More than enough people are called for the number of trials. If there are five trials scheduled, they call more than 60 possible jurors. Trials also don't start promptly. A lot of discussion takes place between the judges and the legal teams before jurors are called. And sometimes a trial doesn't happen at all.

Unusually, that happened to me three times in my first week. The first time, the prosecution decided not to proceed. The second time, the defendant* changed to a guilty plea* at the last minute. The third time, we had no idea what happened: we were about to be brought into the court room and "sworn in"* when instead we were told we could go home.

I waited for between four and six hours each day for three days before being excused. Clearly, lots of waiting around is normal as there were jigsaw puzzles, a dartboard and books in the waiting room to help pass the time. My group were generally quite chatty and friendly—and we had a lot of time to talk to each other. People came from various parts of the region and from all walks of life. (I recognised two people from the town where I live.)

Eventually, I did get called for a trial. Fifteen of us went to the courtroom, from whom twelve were selected. Usually, three are told at random to leave but on that occasion, two jurors claimed a "difficulty" and were excused; which means their judgement may be affected because, say, they knew the defendant or lived very close to the scene of the crime and had heard rumours.

It surprised me to find I was nervous. I knew our decision would be important and I was worried that we might not be able to make the right choice due to inexperience. In fact, the whole system is set up to guide us. The judge put a lot of effort into making sure we knew exactly what was going on: what we should consider, what to disregard and how to reach our verdict. The lawyers for both sides set out their cases in language that we could understand. None of us felt "out of our depth" or confused.

To be honest, I was a bit concerned that my fellow jurors wouldn't take things as seriously as me. There was a lot of joking around in the waiting room and I wondered if some of them were a bit frivolous*. A lot of people were also complaining about the waiting time, about missing work, about their difficult journey to the courtroom etc. Some of them seemed to consider jury service a big inconvenience. But all that changed completely during the trial. Everyone listened attentively* in court, and the discussions over the verdict were entirely serious.

I am embarrassed to admit that I rather arrogantly feared I was cleverer than my fellow jurors. After the first day's evidence, I believed I had noticed something that *only I* would see; something that would mean the man on trial was not guilty. But I was wrong to be worried. When the trial was over and we began our deliberations, several other jurors quickly raised the same issue.

Although I am writing about the experience of being a juror, seeing a trial made me think about it from the other perspective. (As it happens, the man on trial was the same age as me and facing a jury for the first time.)

Firstly, it reminded me of the obvious point that the dock of a courtroom is a place that you never want to find yourself. It's a scary, alien environment for normal people yet so much hangs on the outcome. The man tried before me faced the possibility of going to jail for many years or of going home that very day.

Secondly, if you are ever in trouble you should get a lawyer at the earliest opportunity. The man on trial waived his right to speak to a lawyer before being interviewed by police. That legal advice could clearly have helped him avoid being charged with a very serious offence.

But my main conclusion was that if I somehow ever were on trial I would want to be heard by a jury of my fellow citizens. I was impressed at the orderly way all the jurors managed themselves. In deliberations, everyone got to speak and contributed sensibly. No one attempted to dominate proceedings (except, to some extent, the foreman whom we chose). All the issues that I felt needed to be discussed were discussed. We quite quickly reached a conclusion but before we formally voted we made sure we had properly been through all the evidence and had followed the judge's instructions point by point. No one tried to rush things so we could go home early. We were able to agree unanimously* on a verdict.

Some people in my group served in three trials over two weeks. Twelve people got a murder trial that was expected to last seven weeks. I suppose I was lucky to be dismissed before the usual two weeks' duty was over. But also I was a bit disappointed: doing jury service made me feel like a citizen in full and renewed my gratitude at living in a free, democratic society. I would have been happy to give up a bit of work time to do another trial.

By coincidence, the longest trial in British history ended just as I finished my service. It was an incredibly complex case of financial fraud* in Scotland, that lasted 20 months and required a jury to sit for 320 days of evidence. Such cases are expensive and can collapse because there is a high chance of jurors falling ill or being excused or disqualified over such a long period. So there is still a strong argument that juries may not be best in all circumstances. But I know where I stand on that debate.

Chapter
25

The *"Yuru-kyara"* Challenge

Over the years, I took quite a lot of photos of "characters" that I came across in Japan. The stranger the better, as far as I was concerned. Peopo, the Tokyo Metropolitan Police mascot, was a favourite: a sort of cheerful boy pixie who amused me because he looks wholly unsuited to fighting crime. In Sendai, I remember a creature with an *onigiri* for a head, atop which he wore the distinct crescent moon* helmet of Masamune Date. I wonder what the great warlord would have thought of that. A warrior rice ball!

Only much later did I find out that there was a Japanese term for weird characters (*yuru-kyara*) and that they were a sort of national joke, with certain characters gaining great fame* precisely because they were so odd. Funassyi, the asexual pear fairy, is a Japanese institution while Kumamon, the super-cute bear from Kyushu, is so widely used on merchandise that he (it?) is an economic phenomenon.

In a sense, the *yuru-kyara* craze* is a lot of nonsense. But on the other hand, it requires effort and imagination to create a new character and a little extra something to come up with one that will catch on: a bit of oddball* genius. I still scratch my head at some of the creations that people bring to life but I admire the strange inventiveness of it all. I can remember thinking (and writing in one of my books) that I wouldn't know where to begin in creating such a character.

But that thought bothered me, and I decided I would at least try to create my own Japanese character. I first revealed my ambition to an American friend in Tokyo, Larry, and as chance would have it he had his own idea for a character: Yoko-tsuna, a sumo wrestling tuna fish who fights injustice using his sumo skills.

I was impressed with Larry's clever pun because the best characters have names with some meaning. Apparently, Peopo is short for "people and police" as well as sounding a bit like a police car siren. Hikonyan, the Hikone Castle cat character, combines Hikone with "nyan", the Japanese word for "miaow". Naturally, I resolved that my character would have an amusing and relevant* name.

Ladies and gentlemen, I would today like to unveil ... Igi-Risu!

Igi is a squirrel, of course, but more specifically he's a British squirrel who lives in Japan. And he doesn't find everything to his liking. He is quite often found objecting to things that annoy him because of his different cultural expectations.

I have no talent for drawing so I will have to describe to you what he looks like. Importantly, he is a red squirrel because these were the original native squirrels of Britain. Sadly, they have been largely driven out by grey squirrels (except in Scotland). British people love red squirrels even though many of us have never seen one in real life. Plenty of British people (including me) detest grey squirrels and even refer to them as "tree rats". "Real squirrels are red!" they say. So Igi is red with a bushy tail and furry ears.

But he's not pure squirrel, he's a sort of human hybrid. We'll come to this later but he can do things that squirrels can't do, such as talk and write. (And he doesn't do squirrel things like fill his cheeks with nuts.) So Igi has some human characteristics. His face can look a bit cross*, the way a person's can; his eyebrows sometimes knit* together in disapproval.

It needs to be clear at a glance that Igi is British. I considered giving him an umbrella and a bowler hat*, since that is how Japanese people picture British men. But the fact is no one wears a bowler hat anymore and British men rarely carry an umbrella. So I thought it would be simpler just to give Igi some Union Jack shorts. A bit tasteless maybe but Union Jack shorts were popular when I was growing up in the 1980s.

I expect you will have guessed by now that Igi-Risu is in fact my alter ego*. He's a character version of me, or of *an aspect* of my personality. As it happens, when I was a very small boy my nickname was "Squirrel" and later, when I was a teenager, the house we lived in was named "The Squirrels". So it seems that this character version of me was sort of "fated". Batman was traumatized by bats as a boy, Spiderman was bitten by a spider and I was invested* with the spirit of a squirrel at an early age. So Igi-Risu is also the superhero version of me, fighting against minor inconveniences wherever he goes.

Igi is intelligent, a bit grumpy* and prone to speak his mind even when everyone disagrees with him. Just for example, if he is made to stand at the traffic lights for five minutes he will protest that too much priority is given to drivers in Japan at the expense of pedestrians. The people around him will ignore him or perhaps tell him "It's the rules!" but Igi will answer indignantly that the rules should be changed.

Or he will walk up to politicians during election time and ask them to stop shouting through their megaphones as it is really noisy and irritating. He also gets very cross with Japanese banks because of their terrible service: shutting at 3pm, no branches open at weekends, fees for simple transfers or even for withdrawing your own money. And so on.

Sometimes people will get angry at this interfering foreign squirrel and ask what right he has to criticise Japan. All I can say is that Igi doesn't complain because he dislikes Japan. Quite the opposite. It's because he loves Japan and the Japanese people and wants to make things better for them. If the result is that he is spurned* and isolated, it's a price he is willing to pay.

It seems that *yuru-kyara* need to be cute, and so far Igi may sound like he is rather difficult to love. But he has an endearing way of speaking Japanese badly. He's not a native speaker of Japanese and his little squirrel brain gets confused sometimes. No matter how many times he's corrected, he still thinks you can make a noun into a plural by adding an -s at the end. There's humour in the gap between the earnestness* of Igi's protests and the clumsiness of his language, such as his ardent* "*seijikas urusakunaku suru*" campaign.

Or there was the time he made a poster that he thought neatly distilled* his position on a complicated subject: "*sansei suru no wa hantai!*" And then he made it even shorter for the placard that he carried around town: "*sansei: hantai!*"

Igi doesn't exactly have an age because he's

never celebrated a birthday. He thinks he was born on the 32nd of March but he doesn't actually remember being born so he's not sure. He's an adult but not old. He's male and British but you should be careful not to mention it when he is on one of his campaigns as it will make him angry. He thinks you should be listening to his logical arguments not focussing on his nationality or gender.

He's eccentric, he's cute, he's bold. He's the best I can do. Is he a *yuru-kyara* in full?

Chapter
26

"The Wetherspoons Brexit Test"

In Britain there are a few things that you really can't ask people, even close friends. You can't ask how much someone earns. You can't ask how many sexual partners someone has had. You shouldn't ask how much someone's house cost. And now there is a new one: you can't ask whether someone voted to leave the EU or to remain.

Actually, it would be more accurate to say that you can't ask these things *directly*. It's too blunt*. You can pose "leading" questions to encourage them to reveal information. You could, for example, mention changes to the tax system and see if your friend reveals which tax bracket* he is in (over £50,000 per year and you start paying 40% income tax). You could ask whether he is enjoying being single or whether he had a lot of "luck" in his bachelor days. And, for housing, you can ask obliquely* what "the market" was like when he bought, or what does a "typical" house in his area cost.

If the friend chooses to reveal details about his business, then that's fine (usually, any disclosure* must then be matched: you have to give some info about your situation in return). But if he doesn't want to tell, you have to back off and not press the issue. To continue would be a breach of social norms*.

"Brexit" is slightly different because it's a much newer topic. The rules are not clearly established. For a while, before the referendum* in 2016, people did ask each other how they intended to vote. And for a while afterwards people still continued to ask each other which way they voted. This was unusual because people don't normally ask which party others voted for in a general election. I think it's because the "yes or no" referendum on a single issue was a novel concept to most

UK voters: we had to ask around because we were still figuring it out ourselves, and then we wanted to see if people we respected and liked were on our side of the divide or not.

But three years on the whole situation is too contentious* to be discussed casually. Families fight over it, friends sometimes fall out. The stakes* are high, the future of Britain is being decided. The problem of course is that there is no consensus, and no real "middle ground" on which both sides can agree. The referendum revealed a split that was almost 50-50. Just over half (51.9%) of voters voted to leave, a little under half (48.1%) voted to remain. And the split continues to this day. Commentators used to explain British politics by referring to "haves and have-nots" or in terms of class, gender, race, aspirations* etc. Today, voters are "Remainers" or "Leavers" before all else. We are defined by terms that didn't exist a decade ago.

Normally in a democracy the losing side

concedes* defeat (it has to). That hasn't happened on this occasion. Remainers have continued to insist that there should be a second referendum, which they call a "People's Vote". They say that the first referendum was flawed* because it reduced a complex question to "in or out". They say that the Leave campaign won because it told lies. Quite a lot of Remainers simply believe that Leave voters are too stupid to understand the issue, and that they only voted Leave as some sort of petulant* protest. At the extreme end, I have heard Remainers refer to Leavers as "morons", "racists", "mouth-breathers"* and "Neanderthals".

In turn, I have heard Leavers refer to Remainers as "arrogant", "elitist", "unpatriotic" or even "traitorous"*. So it's a toxic situation and I think you can understand why a British person wouldn't casually ask someone which side he took. It could easily descend into a vicious argument with name-calling*. Even at the best of times, there's little "meeting of minds" across the divide.

Of course, some people openly advertise their views. And of course these are the last people you want to engage on the subject because they are likely to be smugly* self-certain. It's tiresome to talk to people who just insist that they are right and the other side wrong. More commonly, people just hint at their affiliation*. If, for example, someone mentions how much "the make-up of Britain" has changed, there's a fair chance that he is a Leaver unhappy about how EU "freedom of movement" has contributed to mass immigration to Britain (some 3.5 million EU citizens now live here). If you hear someone saying how cheap and reliable his Polish plumber is, he may be a Remainer who sees the same issue—immigration—in a positive light.

A lot of the time people guess, or just assume, that others share their views. It's a cliché that people at London dinner parties bond over their mutual* disgust at Leavers. Broadly speaking, Londoners voted to Remain, as did people in most other big cities. Young people (under 40, say) mostly voted Remain, as did people with university education, wealthier people and Scottish and Northern Irish people. The "average" Leaver is older, working class, and from England, especially the North and the Midlands.

But it is important to remember that these are just indicators, not certainties. For example, Havering is a district of London but almost 70% of people there voted Leave. Even in "pro-EU" Scotland, almost 4 people in 10 voted Leave. Meanwhile, plenty of older people voted Remain because their grandchildren asked them to. ("It's about *my* future, Nan!")

So you should be careful about making assumptions. I was at a party once where someone cheerfully denounced* Leavers, unaware that all five people he was speaking to had voted Leave (or at least I *think* they did, I haven't asked them). Another time, I was having a drink with two friends from university. Both of them had degrees, both had lived abroad, and both were financially secure (i.e. on this evidence they "should" be staunch* Remainers). It amused me that despite this both were passionate Leavers.

I think holidays might be a good indicator where people stand on Brexit. People who go on ski trips to Europe are likely to be Remainers. People who go to Blackpool, the garish English seaside resort, are likely to be Leavers. The problem is that millions of British people go somewhere far less "revealing", such as Spain or Greece.

Finally, I hit on the "Wetherspoons test". Wetherspoons is a chain of pubs that exists across the country. It's very popular for a few reasons. Firstly, it's very cheap (a beer is typically 30% cheaper than other pubs in the area). Secondly, it has a wide selection of beers (my local Wetherspoons often has 12 or more different draught beers available). Thirdly, it doesn't play music, so it's a place for conversation rather than partying. So, it's particularly liked by middle-aged men, such as me, who like beer.

However, there are plenty of people who despise* Wetherspoons. They say that it is "bland"*, because it's a chain, and they don't care that it's a bit cheaper because a pound or two makes no difference to them. They hate the food, which is admittedly rather unexciting, and prefer "authentic" food from restaurants, even if it is four times the price. But the real reason many don't like Wetherspoons, in my view, is that they don't like the customers. Wetherspoons is for the common people: they swear, drink too much beer, talk about football... and voted Leave.

There seems to be a huge overlap between people's attitude to Brexit and their attitude to Wetherspoons. If someone is a Wetherspoons regular in their hometown and seeks out the local branch when they travel elsewhere in the UK, it's highly likely that he is a Leaver. If someone says they wouldn't be seen dead in a Wetherspoons, the chances are he is a Remainer. So this is the technique that I use to "secretly" ask people about Brexit. I drop Wetherspoons into the conversation and see how they react.

My theory is still largely untested, but soon after I came up with it I heard that one acquaintance who used to go to Wetherspoons stopped going after the Brexit vote (he was an avid Remainer). So that seemed to confirm my view. Then recently I was drinking with a Leaver friend in a Wetherspoons in a posh area of London when he said, to my surprise, that he felt "safe" in that pub. I asked him what he meant and he replied it's the only place in the area where he can talk about Brexit without everyone verbally attacking him.

So you can't ask me what position I took. But now you don't have to.

Notes

本文に*をつけた語句の参考日本語訳の一覧です。

1 | Words for Uncommon Situations
めったにない状況を指す言葉

infer	推論する、考え出す（ここでは「造語する」）
prone to...	……する傾向がある
stumble across...	……を偶然見つける
bob	お辞儀する、（頭などを）上下に動かす
get stuck	立ち往生する
stoop	かがむ
trainer	スニーカー、トレーニングシューズ
be horrified	あきれる、ショックを受ける

2 | Mind the Gap(s)
文化の差にご注意を

quirk	癖、おかしな行動
the crook of one's arm	腕を曲げた内側の部分
trousers	ズボン
prevalent	よくある
crumb	かけら
pedestrian	歩行者
prudish	（性的なことに）上品ぶる
vigorously	力強く
bristle	（あごなどの）短く硬い毛
moan	うなる、不平を言う
germ-laden	バイ菌だらけの

3 | Party On, Japan!
パーティーしようよ、ジャパン！

get stung	刺される

intensity	強烈さ、激しさ
cozy	くつろいだ
tiresome	やっかいな
shiver	震える
limp	弱々しい
fizzle	勢いがなくなる

4 | The Treasures of British Cuisine
イギリス料理の宝

topped with...	……を上に乗せた、かけた
moreish	おいしくてあとを引く、もっと食べたくなる
a dash of...	少量の……
Seville orange	サワーオレンジ、セビリアオレンジ、ダイダイ
condiment	香辛料
chunky	(食べ物が)かたまりの入った
relish	(ピクルスなどの入った甘酸っぱい)つけあわせ
tangy	鼻にツンとくる
bland	淡白な
bacon rasher	ベーコンラッシャー、ベーコンの薄切り
brew	ここでは「飲める状態になった紅茶」
be put off	嫌がる
carbonate	炭酸ガスを入れる
crave	切望する
spicy	香辛料の効いた(イギリスのクリスマスプディングには香辛料が使われている)

5 | Ten Japanese Myths
日本にまつわる10の神話

wild	とっぴな、見当違いの
be bemused	困惑する

atop	頂上に
constitutional monarchy	立憲君主制

6 | "Secrets" of the English
イギリス人の「秘密」

formula	方式、決まった形式
hapless	不幸な、哀れな
market stall	屋台
prowess	技量
loose tea leaf	包装されていない茶葉
surge	急激な高まり
interaction	相互作用
infestation	(ねずみ、害虫などが)はびこること
mimic	(笑わせるために)まねる
be outnumbered by ...	……より数が少ない
sensible	分別のある
stingy	けちくさい
demeaning	卑しい、屈辱的な

7 | A Sniffer's Guide to Japan
日本の「匂い」案内

olfactory	嗅覚の
blast	送風、排気、強いひと吹き
circa ...	およそ……、……ごろ(年代とともに用いる)
pump	(気体などを)送り出す、浴びせる
alluring	魅力のある
prolifically	盛んに
intoxicating	夢中にさせる
ambient	あたりに
stink	悪臭を放つ

8	**To Be in England in the Summertime** イギリスで夏を過ごすということ
bare-chested	上半身裸で
sweltering	うだるように暑い
cope	対処する
weigh up...	……を比べてよく考える
dribble	したたる
staple	主要食品
mechanical	自動的な、機械的な
surreal	超現実的な
quasi-	(複合語で) 類似の、準……

9	**The Japanese Have a Word for It** 日本語でなら言えるのに
clumsily	ぎこちなく
schadenfreude	他人の不幸は蜜の味
plus ça change	変われば変わるほど元のまま
kismet	運命
hilarious	とても楽しい
exuberant	極端な、元気にあふれた
malfunctioning	異常な、正常に作動していない
harsh	厳しい、無情な
cormorant	鵜
gullet	食道
learn by rote	丸暗記する
nan	おばあちゃん
flinch	たじろぐ、ひるむ
evocative	(感情などを) 呼び起こす、示唆に富む
endearing	かわいらしい
diminutive suffix	指小接尾辞 (親愛の情を示す)
onomatopoeia	擬声語、オノマトペ

10	**The Things They Ask** みんなが知りたがること
simultaneously A and B	Aと同時にB(である)
bump into...	……にばったり出会う
squiggle	短くくねった線
pictograph	象形文字
let go	自制心を失う、熱中する

11	**Miscellaneous Strange Habits of the English** イギリス人の奇妙な癖
miscellaneous	種々さまざまな
inevitable	不可避の
belly	腹
on the premises	店舗や建物内で
take out...	……を開設する
fondness	慈しみ、愛情
tumble dryer	回転式乾燥機
pop	ひょいと入る
inexhaustible	無尽蔵の
tap	蛇口
soak	びしょびしょに濡らす
miser	けち

12	**Surprise Surprise** びっくりばっかり
be dwarfed by ...	……に比べてあまりに小さい、少ない
raucous	騒がしい
straight-laced	堅苦しい
sober	実直な
sensible	思慮のある
staggering	よろめく、千鳥足の

boisterous	騒々しい
demonstrative	感情をはっきり表に出す
scoff	(がつがつ)食う
at some point	ある時点で
dead end	行き止まり
pitch	ピッチ、(サッカーなどの)競技場
lush	青々とした
nuisance	やっかいなもの
get the hang of...	……をものにする、習得する

13 | The London Olympic "Debacle"
ロンドンオリンピックの「破綻」

flag up	注意を喚起する
retrofit	改装する
The London Legacy Development Corporation	ロンドン・レガシー開発公社
it is not until...that	……して初めて
"freedom of information" legislation	情報公開法
invoke	(法などを)適用・運用する
steward	観客係
dent	解消、改善
affordable housing	手ごろな住宅
the investment arm of the Qatari ruling family	カタール王室の投資部門
obesity	肥満
one-off	一度限りの、またとない
corrective	方法、策
venue	(競技大会などの)会場
balloon	膨れ上がる
whizz	すいすい移動する
confine	制限する

rejoice	喜ぶ
ration	配給

14 | Keeping It Brief
略語のつくりかた

abbreviate	略す
intuitive	直感的な、直感でわかる
dispense with...	……なしで済ませる
juggle	(ボールなどを)巧みに空中であやつる
counties	countyの複数形。(イギリスでは)州
brevity	簡潔さ
ta-ta for now	それじゃまた。ta-taは幼児語で「バイバイ」

15 | The Japan I Didn't Like
ぼくが好きになれなかったニッポン

bump	ぶつける
flippant	ふまじめな
maddening	いまいましい
blithely	無邪気に
ramble	ぶらぶら歩く
bash	ひどく非難する、バッシングする
ward office	区役所
air one's grievances	……の不満をさらけ出す

16 | Perplexities of British Life
イギリス暮らしの悩み

profusion	豊富、ここでは「取れすぎ」
bruised	へこんだ
blemished	傷がついた
ripe	熟した
barrels of beer	ここでは「だぶつくビール」

foolproof	間違えようのない、成功間違いなしの
hangover	二日酔い
sobering	はっとする、我に返る
sneak...out	……をこっそり持ち出す
get round...	……をうまく避ける
vice versa	反対に
clutter	散乱したもの、ごみの山
techie	テクノロジーに通じた人
reciprocal	互恵的な
manoeuvre	巧みに動く
swipe	（カードなどを）読み取り機に通す
bewildering	当惑するような
trainspotter	鉄道オタク
retrieve	回収する

17 | A Journey into Japanese
日本語への旅

sceptical	懐疑的な
mundane	平凡な
deduce	推測する
shame	残念なこと
fall into disuse	使われなくなる
be intrigued	興味をそそられる
crafty	ずる賢い
wean off	やめる
apt	適切な
opine	意見を言う、考える

18 | "Sort of" Equivalents
「どこか」似ているもの

natural state	自然な状態
crumbly	くだけやすい

Notes 193

decent	きちんとした
boldly	大胆に
against great odds	ほとんど無理に思えたのに
interaction	交流
be repulsed by ...	……に嫌悪感を抱く
yeast extract	酵母エキス
won't touch it	絶対に食べない
amulet	お守り、魔よけ
send something hurtling	(石などを)転がす
intensely	激しく
jostling	押し合い
bonding	絆づくり、結びつき
et al.	およびその他の人たち(「and others」を意味するラテン語 *et alia* などの略記)
stretch	拡大解釈、こじつけ

19 | Help! I Am Turning into a Trainspotter
助けて！ 電車オタクになりそう

dismissive	冷淡な、そっけない
flask	魔法瓶
sign up	参加登録する、入隊する
affection for ...	……に対する愛情
sing the praises	ほめちぎる
glaze over	生気を失う
discernible	明確な
be infuriated	激怒している
maroon	えび茶色の
be reminiscent of ...	……をしのばせる
enhance	(質を)高める、(さらに)増す
sleek	(車などが)格好いい、流線形の
overshadow ...	……に勝る、……の影を薄くする
incur	(代金を)発生させる

stare out a window	窓の外を眺める

20 | Best of British Manners
イギリス人の見上げたマナー

wary of...	……に慎重である
prominent	顕著な
altruistically	利他的に
swerve	よける
instinctive	本能的な
admonishment	忠告、注意
take a sip	ひと口飲む

21 | Japanglophilia Cafe
ジャパングロフィリア・カフェ

fancy	食べたいと思う
down-to-earth	地道な、堅実な(ここでは「庶民的な」)
clubber	クラバー(クラブ〈昔でいうディスコ〉の愛好家)
ginkgo nut	銀杏の実
goji berry	クコの実
persimmon	柿
left over	食べ残した
sprout	芽キャベツ
hearty	(食事などが)たっぷりとした
thrifty	節約になる
sprinkle	(液体などを)振りかける
starchy	でんぷん質の
mushy pea	マッシー・ピー(ゆでてつぶしたエンドウ豆)
unsettling	落ち着かない、不安な
Mars bar	マーズバー(マーズ社のチョコレートバー)
culinary	料理の
sliver	細切り

kipper	キッパー（燻製ニシン）
shard	千切り
skewer	串、焼き串

22 | A Collection of Collectives
集合名詞、大集合

final flourish	ここでは「とどめに」
inanimate	無生物の
harness	馬具、引き具
herd	群れ
sinister	不吉な、邪悪な
gnat	ブヨ
vulture	ハゲタカ

23 | The (Unexpected) Dividends of Thrift
節約の思わぬもうけ

by osmosis	徐々に、じわじわと
resurrect	復活させる
perishable food	生鮮食料品（perishableは「傷みやすい」）
playing the banks at their own game	銀行の業務を逆手に取り、顧客が銀行の資金を運用して利益を得ること
be astonished	驚く

24 | The Juror Experience
陪審員の体験

civil servant	公務員
summon	呼び出す
criminal trial	刑事裁判
jury	陪審、陪審員団
impractical	非現実的な
verdict	評決

indignantly	憤然として
in retrospect	今にして思えば
waive	免除する
intimidation	脅し
defendant	容疑者（起訴前）、被告人（起訴後）
guilty plea	有罪の答弁
sworn in	宣誓して裁判にのぞむ
frivolous	ふまじめな
attentively	注意深く
unanimously	満場一致の
financial fraud	金融詐欺

25 | The *"Yuru-kyara"* Challenge
「ゆるキャラ」への挑戦

crescent moon	三日月
fame	名声、有名(なこと)
the *yuru-kyara* craze	ここでは「ゆるキャラ旋風」
oddball	変わり者
relevant	関連した
cross	いらいらした、不機嫌な
knit	（まゆを）寄せる
bowler hat	山高帽
alter ego	分身
invest	与える
grumpy	気難しい
spurn	鼻であしらう
earnestness	真剣さ
ardent	熱心な
distill	（要点などを）抜き出す

26 | "The Wetherspoons Brexit Test"
「チェーン居酒屋」でブレクジットテスト

blunt	無遠慮な
tax bracket	税率区分
obliquely	斜めに、遠回しに
disclosure	打ち明け話
social norm	社会規範
referendum	国民投票
contentious	議論を引き起こす
stake	関わり、利害関係、重大さ
aspiration	抱負、願望、熱望
concede	(敗北などを仕方なく)認める
flawed	欠陥がある
petulant	(子どもっぽく)怒りっぽい
mouth-breather	間抜け、能なし
refer to someone as traitorous	裏切り者と呼ぶ
name-calling	中傷
smugly	ひとりよがりに、うぬぼれて
affiliation	(政治的な)信条
mutual	共通の
denounce	(公然と)非難する
staunch	強硬な、熱烈な
despise	軽蔑する
bland	つまらない、味気ない

Afterword

For many years I used to tell people that I had lived "most of my adult life in Japan". (I hoped it made me seem intriguing.) It was true because I went to Japan straight after university and lived there for most of the next 15 years. But sometime this year I estimate that I reached a tipping point: I have probably, just about, spent as much time in England as in Japan since I turned 18.

The good bit is that it means it's appropriate to mark this juncture with a book about "England and Japan". The bad news, for me anyway, is that it makes it harder to justify my odd behaviour and personal quirks on the grounds that I had lived in Japan for so long relative to my time back in England.

The English, you see, know very little about Japan and I found them willing to believe that any strange habits I had were probably acquired there. (I told them it was a "Japanese idea" to take a photo of a favourite old pair of socks before throwing them away.)

Conversely, I think the Japanese have some big gaps in their knowledge about the English, and some odd ideas about us. We aren't all gentlemen, and rarely carry umbrellas, for a start. In this book, I hope I have given some insights into the reality of my country and my countrymen; not exactly "secrets" but things that aren't necessarily well known.

I do hope the disparate musings in this book are of some interest. I wrote them to deadlines and that means I sometimes had a good idea in advance, only to find when I came to write it up that it didn't work. Sometimes, a worryingly small kernel of an idea turned out to be a decent topic for an article. Sometimes, I had ideas stored up for several columns in advance. One time I was utterly bereft of ideas, sat in front of a blank screen to no purpose for hours on deadline day and finally went for a walk in the hope of inspiration. Then I saw a squirrel in the park and it got me to thinking.

We made some small (and not so small) changes between the articles originally published in the magazine and the versions used for the Japanese version *Mind the Gap*. Then we made a few tiny changes to this English edition for editorial reasons, including adding a whole new piece on the subject the British least like to talk about and which non-British always ask us about (Brexit).

If anyone is irked by such inconsistencies, sorry, but also thanks for being such an attentive reader and congratulations on spotting them. I would be happy to buy you a pint as reward for your diligence. But, as you will know since you have been reading so carefully, the "round" system means you have to buy me back a pint so it's not much of a prize.

The chapters veer from serious to light-hearted with little warning. The format of the essays isn't very consistent. The chapter order is a bit random. Not every joke will be amusing to everyone (except to me, that is). The one thing that I think is consistent is that the pieces are quite hard work for non-native speakers. I am really grateful to anyone who makes the effort and sorry that I am not able to express myself in simpler English.

So I tried to summarise the key lessons from the book: Japan and England are different in some ways and similar in others! I am NOT a trainspotter, however much I talk about train stuff. *Bagpuss* is brilliant (you can watch episodes on YouTube and if you are anything like me, it will turn you back into a child for that short duration). Cormorants are cute and should never have rope slung round their necks and be made to work. If you think really hard you can find good excuses for your eccentric behaviour, such as being really tight with money. The English can be quite weird but don't know it. Japan is really interesting in ways many Japanese don't notice. And a really good way to end something fun is with a *tejime* "hand-clapping" ceremony.

"Yō-o...!" clap, clap, clap...

Profile

Colin Joyce is a British writer and journalist. He worked in Tokyo for 10 years at *Newsweek Japan* magazine and the British newspaper, *The Daily Telegraph*, before a stint as a freelancer in New York. He returned to England in 2010, having lived overseas for over 15 years. He is the author of four books available in English from NHK Publishing—: *How to Japan: A Tokyo Correspondent's Take*; *An Englishman in N.Y.—Bites on the Big Apple*; *Let's England—A Foreign Correspondent Comes Home* and *LONDON CALLING —Thoughts on England, the English and Englishness*. His book マインド・ザ・ギャップ！ 日本とイギリスの〈すきま〉 was released in 2018.

装丁・本文デザイン
尾崎行欧
齋藤亜美
(oi-gd-s)

−

装画
唐仁原多里

−

Notes監修
鍛原多惠子

−

校正
大塚葉子
Carolyn Miller

−

DTP
ドルフィン

−

写真提供
amanaimages
(p.45, p.58)

本書は、NHK出版新書
『マインド・ザ・ギャップ！日本とイギリスの〈すきま〉』
に対応する内容の英文に
"The Wetherspoons Brexit Test"
の章を追加しました。

"Secrets" of England

2019年8月30日　第1刷発行

著者	コリン・ジョイス
	© 2019 Colin Joyce
発行者	森永公紀
発行所	NHK出版
	〒150-8081
	東京都渋谷区宇田川町41-1
	電話　0570-002-046（編集）
	0570-000-321（注文）
	ホームページ　http://www.nhk-book.co.jp
	振替　00110-1-49701
印刷	研究社印刷／近代美術
製本	二葉製本

乱丁・落丁本はお取り替えいたします。
定価はカバーに表示してあります。
本書の無断複写(コピー)は、
著作権法上の例外を除き、著作権侵害となります。

Printed in Japan
ISBN978-4-14-035163-5　C0082

コリン・ジョイスの英文エッセイの本

How to Japan
A Tokyo Correspondent's Take

生活人新書
『「ニッポン社会」入門』を英語で読む。
英紙記者がつづる、
意外な発見に満ちた日本案内。

An Englishman in N.Y.
Bites on the Big Apple

N.Y.に住むことになった
コリン・ジョイスが
切れ味鋭いイギリス英語で
アメリカの虚実をえぐる。

Let's England
A Foreign Correspondent Comes Home

NHK出版新書
『「イギリス社会」入門』を英語で読む。
「階級社会?」「雨ばかりで憂鬱に?」
祖国の謎に挑む。

LONDON CALLING
Thoughts on England, the English and Englishness

サッカー、パブ、
イングリッシュ・ガーデン、
ロンドン俗語などが話題のエッセイ集。
日本語訳付き!

本書 "Secrets" of Englandの日本語版

NHK出版新書 542
**マインド・ザ・ギャップ!
日本とイギリスの〈すきま〉**

日本びいきでも
イギリスびいきでもない。
コリン・ジョイスだけが語ることのできる
ユーモアあふれる「日英論」。